CRITICAL ACCLAIM

"Step-by-step procedures for accomplishing significant and enduring personal changes.... *Be Who You Want, Have What You Want* is a deftly written and superbly presented compendium of insightful advice and practical assistance. It also includes work spaces and exercises that make it truly interactive."

—*Midwest Book Review*

"Guaranteed to fast-track your life.... Chris Prentiss's style is both compelling and entertaining."

—*ReverseSpins.com*

"Brilliant, insightful, and a MUST READ."

—*BackFlap.blogspot.com*

"If I had 5 thumbs, I would put them all up."

—*MensSelfesteem.com*

BE WHO YOU WANT HAVE WHAT YOU WANT

change your thinking change your life

CHRIS PRENTISS

wisdom tree

First published in India in 2010
by arrangement with Power Press, USA.

Reprinted in 2012

ISBN 978-81-8328-163-8

Published by
Wisdom Tree,
4779/23, Ansari Road,
Darya Ganj, New Delhi-2
Ph.: 23247966/67/68
wisdomtreebooks@gmail.com

Interior design: James Bennett

Printed in India

*For those who have less
than they want*

The vision to see,
the wisdom to know,
the courage to do

CONTENTS

MAKING IT YOURS

EXERCISES

ACKNOWLEDGMENTS

I wish to thank my mother, Bea Christiansen, for my most unusual upbringing and for her constant message to me: "You can do it!"

I am also supremely grateful to Nigel J. Yorwerth and Patricia Spadaro of PublishingCoaches.com for their support, friendship, expert coaching, and editing; for shepherding this book through all of its phases to completion; and for bringing about the maximum distribution and sales of my works. Thank you for caring for my work as if it were your own. Patricia makes every writer look better than he or she is. I also thank Nigel for representing my work as my literary agent and being solely responsible for negotiating over twenty-six beautiful foreign editions of my books worldwide, and counting.

HOW TO READ THIS BOOK

The concepts, stories, instructions, and exercises in this book form a program that will enable you to discover the flaws in your thinking that have caused you to be less and have less than you could have had. This program will also help you to remove the limits you have accepted for yourself, allowing you to be who you want and to have what you want. I've included the stories as examples of the concepts in action so you can see the principles at work. The exercises provide you with a way to put the concepts into action in your own life *immediately*. The exercises are of greatest importance.

Much of the information in this book will be new to you. If it were not that way, you would already be who you want and have what you want. Therefore, the following suggestions on how to read this book will be of major benefit to you. Pay close attention to this information. To achieve the greatest benefit from this program, carry out these instructions *precisely*.

Read slowly. Give your mind time to fully absorb the information. Speed-reading will cause you to miss part of what's here. If you find you have read a paragraph or even a sentence quickly, relax and read that part again. Find some way of reminding yourself at the beginning of each chapter that you are to read slowly. I know you are eager to get the payoff I have promised, but reading quickly will slow that process or cause you to miss it entirely.

Make certain you understand every sentence in this book. Sometimes we read words with our eyes that we fail to understand with our minds. *The words in this book call for your full attention and you need to understand them completely.* Use a highlighter to highlight important sentences or paragraphs, or use a pen to underline them. That will make it easier for you to go back and scan the parts you felt were important for you. I have put important words and points in italics. If you are highlighting or underlining, highlight or underline all of those words. Taking notes on what you read will also benefit you greatly.

Several hours after reading a chapter, glance through the pages again. Refresh your memory with the information in the chapter. Think about what you have read. *Make the information your own.*

Review earlier chapters. This will renew and increase your understanding of the concepts. Each time you read a chapter you've read before, the concepts will become clearer as you discover different meanings and new information. The clearer the concepts become, the more capable you will become and the sooner you will bring about what you want in your life.

Do the exercises. Reading this book will give you intellectual knowledge, but that is not enough. To put the intellectual knowledge to work and to receive the maximum benefits from this book, you must do the exercises. *Do the exercises as well as you are able to. They are part of the heart of this book.* Carry out the instructions precisely. You may have reasons that you think justify failing to follow specific instructions. Those reasons are all the same—they are all "reasons for failing to follow instructions." No one reason is better than another and none of them justify not doing the exercises. You are reading this book to bring about a major change in your life. The key to doing that is in doing the exercises thoroughly and with a good heart.

Come to this book prepared to put forth your full effort. Make yourself so familiar with the concepts that they become part of you. React to life in the new ways described within these chapters. Then you will find what you seek, and you will find it more marvelous and abundant than you have ever imagined. You will be going through a major overhaul and the results will keep you smiling for the rest of your days on the planet.

1

REINVENTING YOUR WORLD

Progress is impossible without change; and those who cannot change their minds cannot change anything.
—George Bernard Shaw

I PROMISE YOU THAT BY READING THIS BOOK you will learn how to be who you want and have what you want, and you'll have fun doing it. The big bonus is that you will also learn how to be happy, which is an art in itself.

There is an old saying, "The more you do of what you've done, the more you'll get of what you've got." That saying has merit because doing what you've been doing has brought you to this point in your life where you are who you are and have what you have. If who you are and what you have is what you want, that's perfect. Keep doing what you've been doing and you'll get more of it. However, if who you are and what you have is less than or different than what you want, you'll have to make some changes to get what you want. *You will have to reinvent the way you see your world.*

I say "your world" because each of us lives in a different world. Your childhood was different, your parents or lack of them was different, your experiences were different, your relationships were different, your traumas were different, your health history was different, the life lessons you learned were different, and, as a result, your understanding of how the world works is different from everyone else's. Even if the differences were small, it is those small differences that make all the difference.

Your perception of the world and the way you see yourself in it has created within your mind a concept, a philosophy, of the way you believe things to be. We all have a personal philosophy. Although you may not have ever defined your philosophy, it is fully operative and working in your life every day, all the time. It determines what you believe about the world, about how events and circumstances affect you, and about how you affect them.

Acting on the basis of your philosophy—what you believe to be true about the world and how it works—has primarily created who you are and is responsible for what your life is like today as you read this. You'll learn more about your personal philosophy in chapter 5. For now, here are a few examples of what makes up a philosophy and how that philosophy creates and maintains your view of the world and governs how you respond to events. Some of these examples are part of your philosophy.

It's a dog-eat-dog world.
Don't trust anyone.
Only fools tell the truth all the time.
People are just out for what they can get.
Into every life some rain must fall.
You've got to take the bitter with the sweet.

You can't have it your way all the time.
Bad things happen to good people.
Bad things happen to bad people.
Bad things happen.
I'm not a particularly lucky person.
If it weren't for bad luck, I wouldn't have any luck at all.
God punishes me.
The devil puts traps in my path.
God is mean.
There is no God
Murphy's law: "If anything can go wrong, it will."
or
People are generally good-hearted.
I'm a lucky person.
Things always turn out for the best.
Every cloud has a silver lining.
I expect good things to come my way.
Good things seem to come my way all the time.
I can always see goodness in people.
I can take every situation, no matter how bad it seems, and turn it into good fortune.
Being the best person I can be always brings me benefits.
Every ending contains a new beginning, a new opportunity.
I believe that God exists.
God watches out for me.
God is good.
Everything always turns out for the best.

Take a moment now and see if you can think of a few examples that might define your own philosophy. If you want to, you can borrow from the list above.

You may not be aware of the power of your philosophy to shape your life—how it guides your actions, how it is responsible for the choices you have made in your life, how it has brought you to where you are now—but before you finish this book, you will be fully aware.

HOW YOU SEE

You are not alone in your quest to be who you want and have what you want. Being happy is *everyone's* ultimate goal, no exceptions. That so few of us have achieved it is mainly due to what we learned as children, which is when the major portion of our philosophy was shaped, and how we have lived to this point in our lives. If the people from whom you learned—your family, your teachers, and your friends—didn't know how to achieve that goal for themselves, how could they have taught you to do so? You can relax now; you are about to find out how to change all that.

One of my goals in this book is to help you correct the flaws in your philosophy that are holding you back from being who you want and having what you want. One of the ways to accomplish that begins with changing how you see your world and how you think about what you see.

Here's a simple example. Suppose you and I decided to see a movie. We have been told it is a great thriller, the best one ever made. We go to the cinema, buy our tickets, find seats, and the film begins. We sit there looking for clues—a murder, a theft, a plot, a crime of some kind—but we don't see any of that. After twenty minutes of watching, we are confused and baffled. It's definitely not what we were told to expect. Nothing we are seeing makes sense.

Then the person in the next seat leans over and whispers, "Isn't this a wonderful love story?" Suddenly, everything makes sense. All the events of the film fall into place because we are seeing it for what it really is rather than what we were told it was. We are seeing it with "new sight."

That's the same kind of transformation that will occur as you proceed through this book and start seeing yourself, the world, and its events for what they *really* are rather than what you were told they were. When you change the way you see and interpret events, suddenly everything will be different for you. Everything will make sense. *You will see the past events of your life differently, you will react to new events differently, and you will envision future events differently*. You will love that difference; everyone does. At first, it will be hard to imagine that what you are going to read could be true, but as you continue on, absorbing the information, you'll begin to smile—a lot.

What you'll learn in these pages is that you *do* have the power to actually *reinvent* your world. You are a powerful being, the most powerful being in your life, and you create your future with your thoughts and actions. By changing how you perceive things and how you act upon those perceptions, you *will* change your life.

Throughout this book, you will see statements that will be contrary to what you believe, contrary to what your experience has taught you, contrary to what others have told you, and contrary to any religion in which you may believe. That is to be expected. Because some of what you are about to read will seem impossible or foolish, even ridiculous, it may offend your sensibilities and outrage your common sense—particularly outrage your common sense—causing you to scoff at it, ridicule it, and finally cause you to want to reject it.

My suggestion is that before rejecting it, you take a deep breath and hold it for a moment. Then slowly exhale, opening your mind to accept the idea that what has seemed impossible could be possible, and explore further, asking yourself if you wouldn't like it to be just as you have read.

2

CONSCIOUSNESS

You are a child of the universe no less than
the trees and the stars; you have a right to be here.
And whether or not it is clear to you, no doubt
the universe is unfolding as it should.
—Max Ehrmann, "Desiderata"

IN THE MID-1980s I led workshops in Los Angeles for people whose lives weren't the way they wanted them to be and who were willing to come and listen to me for thirty days to learn how to achieve their goals. I called them Power Workshops. The description of the workshop was "Power: How to Get It, How to Use It, How to Keep It." There were only two rules and they were clearly set out at the beginning of each workshop: (1) Participants had to attend every workshop. (2) Participants had to be on time.

To begin attending the workshop, each person had to make a commitment to honor those two rules. When the door closed at the beginning of each workshop, participants had to be in the room or they were expelled from the workshop, no exceptions. As a result of that rule, between 30 and 40 percent of the workshop participants never made it through the whole program because either they did not attend a workshop or they arrived late.

Those who completed the entire program made such extraordinary gains in their lives that near the end of each workshop some of them would leave their homes to come to the workshop with enough extra time so that if their car broke down, they could walk, take a bus or taxi, or do whatever it took to get to the workshop on time. One girl kept roller skates in the back of her car as her safeguard, another person a bicycle. They were completely committed to attaining their goals, which, of course, was the purpose of the two rules—learning about commitment.

The results the workshop participants achieved were so stunning that, after two years, I discontinued the workshops, sold the building in which I was holding the workshops, and retreated to my home to discover the basic underlying principles that were causing the students to achieve their extraordinary gains. I had recorded all the workshops and had the tapes transcribed into ten large volumes. I studied those volumes for two and a half years. The result is the information in this book, which I have refined and polished over the last twenty years while teaching others those principles along with new principles I learned along the way.

THERE ARE NO COINCIDENCES

Just as those workshop participants changed their lives, you now have the opportunity to change your life. Even though we haven't met, I have total confidence in you. My total confidence stems from the fact that you are reading this book. It's not a coincidence. I do not believe in coincidences, and by the time you finish this book, if I have done my job, you won't believe in them either. What we call coincidences, *accidental and remarkable events occurring at the same time,* are actually circumstances and events that have come into your life to serve a purpose—and that purpose is to benefit you.

We are now starting to touch on a topic that will be of greatest importance to you. How did the *seemingly* coincidental ("accidental and remarkable") event of your getting this book come into your life? If it was not a "coincidence" of some sort, what was it?

The Universe created the circumstances that brought this book to your attention or into your possession.

You are most likely thinking, "What's that you said? The Universe? You've got to be kidding me!"

No, I'm not. At the time of this writing, I am seventy-two years of age, and the single most important piece of information I have ever become aware of is

The Universe is alive, conscious, and aware.

The second most important piece of information I have ever become aware of is

The alive, conscious, and totally aware Universe is completely aware of me.

The third most important piece of information I have ever become aware of is

The totally alive, totally conscious, and totally aware Universe takes care of itself completely. It is totally self-reliant and totally self-sufficient. It is perfect.

As a result of the above three pieces of information, I reached the single most important conclusion of my life, which is

The Universe takes care of me perfectly because I am it.

My son Pax tells me that what I just wrote may be "too much too soon." That may be. Remember, I lost between 30 and 40 percent of my workshop participants because the standards of the workshop were "too much too soon." But you and I have a long way to go to change your life, and we must get on with it if we are to win through to the goal of getting you to be who you want and have what you want. Remember, *I have total confidence in you*. Remember *why* I have total confidence in you: You're reading this and it is not a coincidence; it's a meant-to-be.

UNIVERSAL CONSCIOUSNESS

Everything in the Universe is made of the same energy. The world's most famous equation is Albert Einstein's $E=mc^2$. It basically means that E (energy) equals m (mass) multiplied by the velocity of light squared. *That means that energy and the physical matter of the Universe, including you and me, are different forms of the same thing. You are part of the same energy that is the entire Universe*. It is critically important that you grasp what that means. It's what I said above; you *are* the Universe—a part of it.

The word *Universe* is made up of two Latin words—*uni* (meaning "one") and *versus* (meaning "turned into"). It literally means "one turned into." What was the "one" that those who created our language were talking about, and what did the "one" turn into? I believe the "one" was a vast body of conscious energy that turned itself into "The Universe." This is not so different from the common belief in most religions that in the beginning there was a supreme being (a God) who created the world and the heavens. Don't you find it amazing that those who created our language knew what you've been reading here—that the one (*uni*) turned itself into (*versus*) "The Universe"?

Now, here's the next piece of information, vital information, that will help you understand Universal consciousness and make the changes that are so important to you.

The energy everything is made of is conscious. It's alive. It's aware. The difference between conscious and aware is that one can be conscious but not be aware of something, such as the fact that that the Earth is spinning at the rate of one thousand miles per hour. The Universe is *totally* aware of *everything*, and that includes everything about you. I realize it's difficult to believe that stars and stones are conscious, that they are made of *the same* energy you are made of. You may now be thinking, "That is a ridiculous notion" and "Any book whose assumption is that everything in the Universe is alive, conscious, and aware cannot be of any great value. I have never seen a conscious stone!" I'll see what I can do within the covers of this book to extend the boundaries of your reason to include this wondrous information so you can enter into this magical world of possibility, leaving behind all that has held you back from being who you want and having what you want.

Just as you and everything in the Universe are part of the same Universal energy, so you also share Universal "consciousness." Where does your "consciousness" come from? Scientists say that consciousness arises when a complex organism, such as a human being, comes into existence, and that there is no consciousness that exists outside of a complex biological organism. They say, for instance, that a stone has no consciousness, but with a complex organism, suddenly, there it is!

What a magic trick—something from nothing. Of course, given a little thought, the idea is ludicrous. Something from nothing? I don't think so. You can take the entire world of physics with all of its macrocosm and microcosm, its quantum mechanics and nuclear physics and reduce it to one word: *energy*. It's *all* energy. Scientists say that if you can't measure it, weigh it, or see it, it doesn't exist. Well, no one has ever seen energy. We can see its effects, but not "it." Nevertheless, we know energy exists. *Energy is all there is*, and everything is made of it, including you and me.

Scientists also say that life *only* exists within a biological form. They say life doesn't exist and, suddenly, with a biological form, life comes into existence—another magic trick. How foolish it is when you think about it. Life from no life? It would be like trying to illumine a lightbulb without electricity first existing. Just because we create a lightbulb does not mean it will glow with light. In fact, it will not glow at all unless electricity is first present.

The same thing is true for consciousness that is true for life; neither can come into being within a biological form *unless consciousness and life first exist*. A biological entity can partake of life and consciousness once they are available, but that entity doesn't *create* life or consciousness by coming into existence any more than a lightbulb creates electricity by coming into existence. In other words, we have life and consciousness because it already exists in the Universe. To me, it is evident that consciousness exists in the Universe simply because you and I have consciousness and you and I are part of the Universe.

CHANNELING INFORMATION FROM THE UNIVERSAL CONSCIOUSNESS

You have been chosen to exist, and more than just to exist—*you've been chosen to share in the Universal consciousness*. Do you think you have all of the consciousness that the Universe has? Of course not. I have some, you have some, and others have some.

Your consciousness partakes of the Universal consciousness in much the same way that a lightbulb partakes of the pool of electricity. It draws from it. We like to take credit when we get a new idea, as if we originated the idea in our brain, but what we actually did was no less extraordinary: we *channeled* the idea. We used our key to unlock the fount of Universal wisdom and information. That you have a key is indisputable; every time you have ever gotten a new idea or thought of something new, you used your key to unlock the fount of Universal information.

You use your brain much as you would use a radio crystal; you tune in different frequencies. When you need an idea about how to accomplish or create something, you think about the subject and soon a flow of information from the Universal bank of information comes in the form of ideas.

It seems as if you are manufacturing those ideas in your

brain, but that's an illusion. Your brain, in some ways, is like a computer, but in one extremely important way it is completely different. You may already know that you can only get out of a computer what you put into it. There's a common saying with computer buffs: "Garbage in, garbage out." That means that you can only get out of a computer what you put into it. A computer cannot manufacture new information. That's the difference between our brain and a computer. We can put into a computer everything there is to know about the physical description of a tree, but the computer will never be able to come up with the unique concept of an apple. We, however, can channel the concept of an apple from the Universal storehouse of information.

In our time, there have been many new and exciting inventions never dreamed of years ago. Suddenly, people conceived of them and then created them. The ideas came into their minds; they channeled them. It is a daily occurrence for people in different parts of the world to conceive of the same ideas at the same time. Scientists are regularly working on the same new concepts in many different parts of the world. They race to see who can come up with the final solution to the same problem to beat out the competitors who are also working on the problem.

Think about the instances of children creating things and doing things far beyond the capability of other children their age. We call them geniuses and child prodigies. It would not be understandable or even conceivable that those children could perform those amazing feats unless we realize that they are channeling the information from the Universe. Wolfgang Amadeus Mozart was composing music at age five, and he certainly was not able to do that because he had spent years laboriously studying musical composition. He was extremely prolific in his lifetime, composing over six hundred works. Where did all that music come from? He was channeling it.

Thomas Edison patented more than a thousand inventions. When he was stumped for an idea, he would sit in a chair, hold a ball bearing in each hand, and rest his arms over the chair's arms. He placed metal pie plates on the floor below his hands. He would then allow himself to relax and get to the point of sleep but not go to sleep. If he did begin to fall asleep, his hands would relax and the ball bearings would fall down, hit the plates, and the sound would awaken him. He would then write down the ideas that had come to him. Edison was channeling.

You can also channel, and you do it all the time. Every time you think of something you've never thought of before, you are channeling. Now that you know how Edison did it, you can do the same thing. You can even make up your own method. The information that you *can* do it is what's important. When you need an idea about how to do anything, get quiet and relaxed and think about what it is you need to know. Then the flow of ideas will come. Be patient and let it happen. Sometimes it takes a little while, but it always works.

THE GREATEST FORCE, THE GREATEST HONOR

Knowing that you are part of the Universe and that the Universe is aware, acutely aware, of you is more empowering than any other single aspect of your life. Suppose it were true. Think what it would mean. It would mean that *the most powerful force that exists is aware of you*, and it is as concerned for your welfare as it is for its own because you *are* its own. This knowledge will alter your life in ways that will amaze and delight you once you come into the full realization of what it means. Being part of the Universe is the greatest honor anyone can have. It's better than king, queen, shah, emperor, supreme ruler, prince, president, or any other title you can conceive of.

In addition to the precious gift of consciousness and the ability to channel new ideas, another gift from the Universe is that you can communicate with it. You may not be aware that this is possible, but before we are finished here, you will do it regularly. In fact, you are doing it now with the thoughts you think, the actions you take, and how you are being at every moment. If you touched one of your shoulders, you would be aware of it because your shoulder is part of you. In the same way, the Universe is aware of your thoughts and actions, of how you are being at every moment *because you are part of it.*

Not only are you communicating to the Universe, but the Universe is also communicating with you. The Universe communicates with you by bringing events into your life. That is its method of communication. And these events are always for your benefit. This book is an event in your life, stubbing your toe is an event, losing a parent or guardian is an event, having a bicycle accident is an event, getting a raise at work is an event, finding a mate is an event, and, yes, the holocaust, 911, and the tsunami that killed over two hundred thousand people in Thailand were all events, along with a day when you were greatly embarrassed as a child.

Those events almost certainly seemed to you to be without purpose, certainly without conscious purpose on the part of the Universe—although they may have had an impact on your life, particularly if you were part of those events or if someone close to you was part of those events. But all events, all communications from the Universe, have a purpose. Not only that, but all events in your life were and are for your total and complete benefit. In fact, they were the best possible events that could have happened. I know it's a bit much right now to think that they were, but we are just getting started. As you work with the concepts in this book, you will come to see the Universe in a completely different way. You'll be living in a Universe where you will understand all these connections and be able to use them to your great advantage.

What has gone before in your life has most probably convinced you that the statement "Everything that happens to me is the best possible thing that can possibly happen to me" is not true and cannot be true, and that a book based in part on that premise is not going to do you much good. It may seem futile to even attempt to put that concept to the test. But this is a new day. We have begun a new century and a new millennium, and you may discover in reading this book that it is your time to take on a new belief that will bless your life from this time onward.

In later chapters, you'll read more about how the Universe communicates with you through events and how you can use that information to create the life you want. For now, just begin to get used to the idea that *every event in your life has been a communication to you from your Universe. It's been a deliberate, calculated, and personal event with the intention of bringing into your life a circumstance that would be of the greatest possible benefit to you at that moment.*

That is going to take some getting used to because of the way you're accustomed to perceiving events, but the effort is startlingly worth it. Besides that, it's true.

FROM WONDER INTO WONDER

Everything is a manifestation of the consciousness and energy of the Universe—you, me, the book you're holding, the air you're breathing, everything. Lao Tzu, a Chinese sage who lived about twenty-five hundred years ago, when speaking of the consciousness of the Universe, its life force, which he called Tao, said:

> The Tao that can be spoken of is not the eternal Tao.
> The name that can be named is not the eternal name.
> The nameless is the origin of Heaven and Earth.

He was saying that by whatever name we call "it," it's just a name we made up to be able to talk about it, but it's not the real name. Nor is it "it" because the real name is unknowable. I call it "the Universe," and I refer to it as "All-That-Is." The entire Universe is one huge mass of energy, and it manifests itself as everything that exists. I capitalize *Universe* for the same reason other people capitalize *God*, out of respect. I do not think of God or the Universe as an entity bound by form or a body but as All-There-Is—literally, a vast, conscious energy.

Witter Bynner, an author interpreting Lao Tzu's work in a book entitled *The Way of Life According to Lao Tzu,* reports the great sage as saying, "Whether a man dispassionately sees to the core of life or passionately sees the surface, the core and the surface are essentially the same, words making them seem different only to express appearance. If name be needed, wonder names them both. From wonder into wonder, existence opens."[1] That sums up the way I feel about life: *"From wonder into wonder, existence opens."*

The fact that something has held you back from experiencing that wonder and from being who you want and having what you want is evident or you wouldn't be reading this book. To remove whatever that something is, you'll have to give up some of what you now believe to be true that is not true. And you'll have to come to believe some things that you now believe are not true which are true, such as what I've written above.

Acting on the basis of what you *believed* to be true about the Universe but what was not true, rather than acting on the basis of what *is* true, has caused you to be less and to have less than you could have had. Once you find out what has held you back and change it, it will be as if you've been driving backwards in a car all your life and you've suddenly discovered there are gears that make it go forward and fast! This is a great adventure, totally captivating and completely rewarding.

EXERCISE NUMBER ONE

Channeling New Ideas

Find a quiet place where you will be undisturbed for at least fifteen minutes. Sit down with this book and read the instructions for the next exercise, Exercise Number Two, "Learning to Be Happy."

Now that you have read Exercise Number Two, sit quietly and channel ideas for that exercise. Think of the pleasurable things you would like to do. Let your imagination roam freely. It may seem as if you are using your imagination, as if you are creating things to think about, but what's really happening is that you are channeling ideas from the Universe. Get the feeling of doing that. Stay open and experience what a good feeling that is.

When you have gotten the ideas you want for your pleasure exercise, write down what you have chosen to do on the page provided at the end of this chapter under the heading "Pleasure Exercise #1." When you are ready, complete your pleasure exercise, following the instructions in Exercise Number Two.

EXERCISE NUMBER TWO

Learning to Be Happy—Pleasure Exercise #1

A major goal of this program is that you be able to experience happiness, joy, ecstasy, or whatever you feel when doing something that gives you pleasure. Therefore, the goal of this exercise is to treat yourself to a half hour of pleasure.

Perhaps you'll choose walking in the hills, on the beach, or in a favorite park. Perhaps you'll go to some favorite spot and sit and read. Maybe there's a friend you want to visit or a long-awaited fun event you want to enjoy. Perhaps there's a sport you love to participate in. If the sport you participate in or the friend you visit disappoints you, or if the book you read is less than completely satisfying, pick another pleasure exercise. If you allow problems or other unpleasurable thoughts to intrude and spoil your half hour of pleasure, gently bring your awareness back to your goal—to enjoy a full half hour of pleasure—and begin again.

If you find you have had many negative thoughts intrude upon your half hour, start over, perhaps choosing another pleasure exercise. If you take a day or weekend off to go somewhere, while you're away set aside a special half hour to fulfill this exercise. *Giving yourself pleasure is an art that can be learned*. When you are finished with this program, you will have acquired that art.

In Exercise Number One, you have generated ideas for what you want to do during your half hour of pleasure and written down your choice on the page at the end of this chapter under the heading "Pleasure Exercise #1."

To begin this exercise, say aloud: *"I, [say your name], give myself permission to enjoy a half hour of pleasure."* The second step is to treat yourself to your half hour of pleasure at the time of your choosing.

When you have completed your pleasure exercise, write the date that you completed it and a brief summary of what happened, how you felt, and any other special thing you care to write about under the heading "Pleasure Exercise #1." If you had to choose another pleasure exercise because your half hour was spoiled by an unpleasant event, write that down also. Be thoughtful in what you write.

Now, we need to have an understanding here, you and I. This exercise is important—very important. You are to fulfill it as though it were the most important task of your life. That means you are to *really* enjoy a *full* half hour of pleasure. I want you to be happy. (This is so important that I have written a whole book on the subject called *Zen and the Art of Happiness*. It's a small book, but it's very effective.) You can absolutely learn to be happy, and I intend that you will have done so by the time you finish this book.

Complete the two exercises in this chapter before going on to chapter 3. That means you are not to read ahead at all before you have completed these two exercises.

Pleasure Exercise #1:

Date completed: ______________________________

3

FIRST LIGHT FROM THE LODESTAR

Happiness is when what you think,
what you say, and what you do are in harmony.
—Mahatma Gandhi

A LODESTAR IS A GUIDING LIGHT—a light you can look to with complete assurance, an ever-burning, bright beacon guiding you safely and with total success. The information, concepts, and insights in *Be Who You Want, Have What You Want* are to be your lodestar. Following your lodestar will create within you an inner certainty, a way of being, that will lead you to the attainment of that which you desire.

Whatever you now do, whatever you now believe, whatever your current circumstances may be, you are perfectly equipped and fully capable of fulfilling your needs and desires. You are about to have it just the way you want it.

The moment you were conceived, you began storing information in your memory. Your memory now contains everything you've ever read, heard, seen, imagined, and experienced. Everything new that you perceive is sifted through your memory to see how it fits in with all that has gone before so you can determine how you should act upon it. This book will provide you with new information to add to your memory that will cause you to act differently as your life unfolds, as you are confronted with new opportunities and new events.

THE MIRROR

The world around you—its people, places, and events—is a mirror. It shows you "Who You Are." It is of major importance that you fully understand and clearly picture this concept in your mind. The following examples will assist you in doing this.

Imagine a woman whose mind is very precise and ordered. Imagine that she is intelligent, neat in her habits, friendly, hardworking, and honorable. If you saw her home, it would be neat, clean, cheerful, nicely furnished, comfortable, and in good repair. You would see "Who She Is" mirrored there. If she performed a task, you would see "Who She Is" mirrored in her work. It would be well done and she would finish the task. If you asked her friends about her, you would hear "Who She Is" mirrored in their descriptions of her. Everything about her—the way she carries herself, the way she dresses, the words she speaks, her actions—all mirror "Who She Is."

In your own life, if you were to critically observe where you live, your clothing, your possessions, your friends, your social situation, your financial situation, your love relationships, your physical condition, and everything you said and did, it would be as if you were looking into a huge mirror. It would show you "Who You Are." Suppose you purchased a small item and the change you received from the salesclerk was five dollars too much. Your immediate reaction, whether you kept the money or gave it back and how you later felt about your actions, would all mirror "Who You Are."

Suppose that you were involved in a highly emotional argument. How you conducted yourself would show you "Who You Are." Did you lose control, become vulgar, nasty, and abusive, or did you remain calm and polite? Suppose you had just won a race. Imagine all the excited spectators, cheering, shaking your hand, congratulating you. They are all mirroring your victory. Suppose you had won the same race, but you had cheated and some of the spectators knew it. Their angry protests, their hissing and booing would clearly mirror "Who You Are."

Scientists today are showing us another dimension to this mirror. They are proving, over and over again, that our physical bodies mirror what's happening with our thoughts and feelings. Negative emotions, like depression or anxiety, have been shown to affect our immune system. Stress impedes wound healing. Fear or distress before surgery is related to things like longer hospital stays, more complications, and more rehospitalization. Stress and anxiety cause our brains to release chemicals that put lines in our faces and tear us down emotionally and spiritually. Those are just a few of the ways that our feelings are mirrored in our body.

Take a few minutes now and see your current circumstances—your physical condition, your emotional condition, your possessions, your financial condition, where and how you live, your relationships, the situations surrounding your life, and the way you believe other people see you—as mirrors showing you "Who You Are." This is an important step, so don't flinch from doing this thoroughly. Put this book down and visualize that now.

Because you are reading this, you know that there needs to be improvement in the conditions of your life. Although it may be difficult for you to objectively look at your life as mirroring "Who You Are," it is essential that you begin to look at your life in that way. The world actually *is* a mirror, and as you change, you will see everything around you changing as well, mirroring your changes.

THAT'S TOUGH

Because the Power Workshops I held in the mid-1980s were so successful, I was interviewed on many radio and television shows to talk about the concepts of the program. Several days after I had been interviewed on a radio show, a man named Ralph telephoned to say he had heard the program and wanted to know more about the Power Workshop I was holding at that time. We talked for a while about the various situations in his life. He told me that he disliked his work and that his marriage seemed to be one continuous quarrel. He said his home was a small, poorly furnished apartment. His income was too small to meet the needs of his large family and he had few possessions. He felt that he had no control over the outward circumstances of his life, that he was stuck, and that he couldn't find a way out of his predicament.

Then he asked where I was holding the workshop. When he estimated that it would be a one-hour drive each way, he said, "Gee, that's tough. I don't think I want to do that." I responded, "Ralph, from what you've told me about your life, the drive to the workshop should be easy in comparison to keeping your life the way it is—*that's* tough!"

This mission of change you are considering for yourself is tough to carry out. But won't it be even tougher to live the rest of your life not being who you want and having what you want?

The changes you are going to make so that you can be who you want and have what you want are *internal* changes. Changing *the way* you see things is much easier than changing the things you see. For instance, if you want to see everything in the world as yellow, you can get a lot of yellow paint and a brush and start painting, or you can put on yellow sunglasses. When you put on yellow sunglasses, the whole world becomes yellow instantly. The moment you make the internal changes necessary to obtain your goal, the outside world changes instantly. There is a major difference between putting on sunglasses and making internal changes, though; while sunglasses can break, the changes you are going to make can be permanent.

The circumstances you need to make these internal changes are already in place. You currently see them as "problems." Is that a surprise? They are part of your life and are what I call "workout situations." These are situations that are in your life for one purpose only—so you can gain wisdom, information, understanding, and strength by working your way through them. Your job is to recognize them with "new sight."

FOR YOUR TOTAL AND COMPLETE BENEFIT

Imagine for a moment that the Universe is your parent, an all-wise, all-knowing, totally powerful parent who loves you completely—a parent who can do anything and accomplish everything. Also imagine that your parent knows the past, present, and future. Most important, imagine that at all times your parent wants to benefit you *in the maximum amount possible*.

Your parent (the Universe) wants you to be strong, but not just by snapping its fingers and making you strong. You wouldn't feel any sense of accomplishment if you became strong in that way, so your parent brings circumstances into your life that will cause you to use your own strength and thereby become stronger.

Suppose that your parent wants you to be wise. Your parent won't just give you wisdom but will provide you with circumstances from which you will gain wisdom. If your parent wants you to be less arrogant, it doesn't just give you a dose of humility. It will create a situation in your life that will cause you to feel humility and recognize its value. The Universe always prospers the humble and brings down the arrogant. It's a Universal law. Sometimes those experiences hurt us, take something from us, or shame us, but they always occur for our total and complete benefit.

Imagine the Universe as a total awareness and a supreme consciousness that is completely aware of you and your circumstances. Imagine that it has taken you under its wing to love, protect, nourish, encourage, and guide you, giving you lessons that will benefit you in the maximum amount possible. That's exactly what "workout" situations are.

After a lifetime of seeing problems as bothersome, troubling difficulties, being able to see the same problems as beneficial workout situations that have been brought into your life for a purpose will be a welcome change. Breaking your old habit of seeing these situations as problems may at first be difficult, but *you can do it.*

When you have obtained the information you are meant to learn from these workout situations, you will cause them to pass out of your life. In kindergarten or first grade, you learn that one plus one equals two. You don't get that in college because you already know it, and you don't need that lesson any longer. It's the same in the Universe; once you get what you need from a workout situation, it passes out of your life, never to return.

If you have experienced recurring situations in your life that are unpleasant, know that there is something you are supposed to be getting from those situations that you have not been getting—and that the moment you get it, those situations will pass out of your life, not to return. Develop the awareness that problems, difficulties, and obstacles are situations in your life that are there for the purpose of helping you be the person who can have what you want and be who you want. They are also mirrors that reflect "Who You Are" and will change as you change.

AN ACT OF COURAGE

The same principles that govern physical power also govern mental power. Body builders achieve their powerful bodies by working out, by "pumping iron," which means they lift heavy weights over and over again. There's a saying among body builders: "No pain, no gain." That means if you're failing to use your muscles to the point where they hurt, you're failing to tear down muscle tissue and rebuild it with new, stronger muscle tissue. Likewise, the situations in your life that will provide you with your mental workout will not be easy to overcome, but by using your determination to overcome the difficulty, you'll build strength, gain awareness, and increase your capability.

Welcome difficult situations. Use them to see "Who You Are" and to gain the valuable information and wisdom they hold for you. Resolve to face obstacles rather than to sidestep them. That is an act of courage. Courage is only necessary when you are feeling fear. Here is a little secret, a little pot of gold at the end of the rainbow: You have enough courage to face even your greatest fear. The Universe, in its great wisdom, does not bring a fearful situation into your life without supplying you, at the same time, with enough courage to face it.

Start believing that problem situations arise *purely* for your benefit. How do you start believing? When a problem or a difficult situation arises, say to yourself, as if you already believed it: "This is for my benefit." Your beliefs, like everyone else's, are based on your experiences—on what you know. By pretending and acting as if you truly believe that everything happens only for your benefit, you'll soon see new results that come from acting on that belief; and based on those new experiences, you'll discover that it is actually true—*then* you'll believe it.

In the beginning, if you encounter a major problem, you're likely to react by saying, "This is for my benefit? That's impossible!" But that major problem is simply there to tell you that you need to make some major changes or that within the situation there is the opportunity to learn something of major importance. Most of the time, when something happens in your daily life, you see it only for what it appears to be and fail to see it for what it actually is: an opportunity for benefits to be gained—benefits of information, wisdom, strength, self-awareness, and personal growth.

If an event takes place that is threatening to you in some way, how you react during and after the event will reveal to you "Who You Are." After the incident is over, if you sit quietly and watch a replay in your mind of what happened, you will learn a lot about yourself.

Here's an exaggerated example of how a situation can lead to that change in perspective and greater self-awareness. Let's say that you want to return an item you recently purchased that turned out to be defective. You go to the store where you purchased the item but find you have forgotten to bring your receipt. The girl at the register tells you she cannot give you a refund without the receipt. Let's say you press the argument, become angry over the clerk's repeated refusal to give you a refund, become very abusive, and use a great deal of vulgarity. The clerk bursts into tears, but you never let up for a moment in your abuse. The argument escalates until the security force escorts you to the sidewalk.

Later on, after you have calmed down and thought about it, you can see that you were asking the clerk to do something she did not have the authority to do. You would see that you were intolerant and unreasonable, you lost control, you embarrassed yourself with your vulgarity, and you were inconsiderate. Your actions of the day were mirroring "Who You Are." If you could see what the clerk thinks of you and what the other customers and the security guards think of you, you would see yourself mirrored in their thoughts.

If you viewed a replay of every situation where you behaved in the way that you just read about, you would soon realize that your behavior wasn't helping you solve a problem at all but was actually contributing to making more of a problem. You might feel shame and remorse. Your self-image might be hurt. If you reviewed your actions every day, it wouldn't take long for you to begin behaving in a new way, a way that would please you when you replayed the scene in your mind.

It's important that you keep in mind that when this program gets tough, you're still on the right track, just a tough track. Your job is to keep on proceeding as if everything that happens is for your benefit. In the next little story, you will see that Caleb took that advice to heart, and it's that idea that propelled him out of his old way of doing things into a life where he is who he wants to be and has what he wants to have.

FROM WISHY-WASHY TO DETERMINED

I met Caleb and his wife, Susan, many years ago when they were both in their early twenties. Caleb was a fairly good carpenter and made a modest income doing odd jobs. He had a winning smile, a good disposition, and a boyish attitude that people liked. However, Caleb lacked assertiveness and had a general weakness that manifested itself in a wishy-washy attitude and a lack of determination in most areas of his life. Consequently, there was unhappiness, bickering, and quarreling mixed in with the good times.

He and Susan shared one small room in the back of his parents' house. It was hardly a peaceful existence because of the considerable traffic through their room whenever anyone went to or from the garage and garbage bins in the backyard. Caleb and Susan had difficulty paying their bills, and their credit cards were always charged to the maximum limits. Their spending was out of control. They owned a few pieces of furniture, the tools Caleb used for his carpentry, and two heavily financed cars.

In those days, their lives were characterized by an inability to have things the way they wanted them and an overall instability. Other people and outside events seemed to control them. Caleb felt locked in by his meager earnings and powerless way of life. His struggle to maintain his credit and back-room lifestyle was less than successful. Caleb told me of an incident from his childhood that summed up his general way of being.

In Caleb's neighborhood, there lived three tough boys who liked to pick on Caleb and some of the smaller boys. Since he was afraid of them, he let them do it. One day, one of the boys wanted to have some fun by beating him up. I remember Caleb telling me how the blood spurted out when this boy finally punched him on the nose and broke it. After the incident, Caleb enrolled in a karate class and in four years learned how to defend himself well. I asked him if he had then settled up with the boy who had broken his nose.

"No," he said. "After the boy broke my nose, they left me alone, and that's all I ever wanted from the beginning." Caleb thought he had learned a valuable lesson—how to win by losing.

Shortly after I met Caleb, I asked him if he would like to radically alter his lifestyle by following an unusual training program. I told him it would be a difficult path, and a long one, and that because of all that had gone before in his life, there was a possibility that he would see the effort required as too great and would quit. But I also told him that his life would radically improve if he kept with the program. After a long discussion, he agreed to make the effort.

Almost immediately, Caleb's first workout situation arose. His wife was a blond, suntanned native Californian. She was delightfully attractive and drew the attention of many men. Caleb had no idea how to deal with this other than to suffer through it. One day he came to me in a distressed state and blurted out: "A man sent Susan a negligee with an invitation that said, 'Let's get together.' When she put it on, you could see right through it! I could tell she loved it."

Caleb was hurt and distressed by Susan's reaction. His win-by-losing lessons had poorly prepared him to handle the situation. I reacted by saying, "Wonderful! This is the perfect situation for you." I told Caleb that this was a situation hand tailored to bring about the best result possible. I told him to go to Susan and ask her to give him the negligee, then to find the gift giver and return it to him, telling him that he, Caleb, was the only one who could give his wife such an intimate gift. He was to do all this in a straightforward, assertive manner but without being combative about it.

As you can imagine, this was a radical change from Caleb's usual it's-okay-to-push-me-around attitude. Although Caleb is of average height and physically fit, he was frightened. I asked him to call upon his courage, and I described what might occur if he failed to act—his wife might accept the man's invitation!

Caleb acted. He went to Susan and asked for the negligee and the name of the gift giver so he could return it along with his demand that the man never do such a thing again. Susan was thrilled! Her timid husband was being manly—

and over her. She fully cooperated.

Caleb telephoned the man, identified himself, and asked for his address so he could come and see him. The man, sensing Caleb's determination and wanting to avoid any possibility of a meeting with an angry husband, refused to tell Caleb where he lived. For three days, Caleb tried to find him, but the man had stopped answering his phone and had an answering machine taking messages. Caleb left many messages, all of which went unanswered. Susan was excited by Caleb's bold and unusual behavior and treated him like a king. Caleb realized that Susan was mirroring the change in his behavior. He loved it!

EVERYTHING IS CONNECTED

For the next six months, rain or shine, six days a week, I met Caleb at 5:30 a.m. and, as part of his training program, coached him for an hour. It seemed at first that during that hour he was learning more about his trade of carpentry than learning about a new way of life, but he was really learning to be the kind of person he needed to be in order to have what he wanted to have and to be who he wanted to be. He learned how to drive in a nail without leaving a hammer mark on the wood, how to make exact corners, how to sand wood to a satin finish, how to leave the job neat and orderly, how to care for his equipment, how to get to his jobs on time, and how to work with the correct attitude, thinking the right thoughts. In the evenings, we met and talked about life, people, events, death, love, greed, passion, power, history, the future, philosophy, and the day's happenings.

Ever so gradually, Caleb began to see that the way he drove a nail into a piece of wood was connected to the way he signed his name on a piece of paper. That the way he took care of his tools was connected to the way he felt about himself. That getting to work on time every day was connected to how he walked, which was connected to being a good friend, which was connected to how he drove his car, which was connected to paying his bills, which was connected to waking up with a smile, which was connected to eating, which was connected to being fit, which was connected to sleeping, which was connected to playing, which was connected to the manner in which he spoke to Susan, which was connected to having all that he wanted. And, most important, he learned that this was all connected to how he saw himself. He began to see that everything was connected to everything else. Everything he did reflected a way of being—*his way of being*. As he improved in one area, all the other areas improved as well.

As Caleb followed the program, he grew ever stronger, but he had two habits that were seriously slowing him down—he consumed a lot of beer and regularly smoked marijuana. I told him that to shift into a condition of full power and awareness, he had to keep his future free from those influences. Since most of his friends were using drugs and alcohol, it was a hard rule for him to follow. There were a few setbacks as Caleb's old lifestyle claimed him for a night, but gradually the effects of his new training took over and he gave up drugs and alcohol completely.

One and a half years after Caleb started the program, he owned over one and a half million dollars of real estate with good, solid equity, including his own home. He drove his own fully paid-for Mercedes and had two other cars as well. He amazed everyone who had once known him as the insecure, incapable "weak kid on the block." A few years later, he owned his own construction company and had many people working for him. Now he vacations regularly at exotic places around the world, and he goes where he wants to go, when he wants to go, and stays as long as he wants to stay. He has recently begun building a vacation home on the beach in Hawaii. He is in control of his life, which is now characterized by comfort, satisfaction, happiness, and the total knowledge that he can influence the course of his life by how he is being at every moment.

Additionally, Caleb is in superb physical condition and recently began competition athletics. He remains free from drugs and alcohol, and his winning attitude is his trademark. The many people in his circle of friends love him for his generosity, his quick laugh, his enthusiasm, optimism, and overall state of well-being.

CHANGING THE WORLD AROUND YOU BY CHANGING YOURSELF

Early one morning as I was writing this, Caleb telephoned to tell me he had been thinking of his earlier days. Many months had passed since I had spoken to him. The conversation went like this:

"You know, Chris, in those early days, before we met, it was like I was spinning. You know how a little kid gets in the middle of a room and spins till he gets dizzy and falls down? It was as if I had always had all the control dials and the stuff that made things work, but I didn't know how to work them. There was something standing between me and them—

something I had put there. I didn't have conscious control of the dials. I was just going through the motions without being in control of my life."

"What did you feel then, Caleb?"

"A grind in my stomach. I still get it whenever I think of those days. I feel it now just talking about it."

"How is your life different for you now?"

"I've grown ten trillion times! I'm aware of myself and my place in the world. When we met, I had all that I have now—you know, my capability and all that—I just didn't know how to use it. What you helped me do was consciously change the world around me by changing myself—to take active steps to create new situations. At first, they all seemed like experiments to me. Some of those experiments originally seemed like failures but ended up to be wonderful states of change. Later, I began to repeat actions that were successful in order to create more and more successes for myself."

"Are you always in control now?"

"No. Sometimes I get into a situation that's too much for me and I begin to 'spin out' like I used to."

"What do you do then—walk away from it?"

"No, of course not! I go back to the teaching you gave me and ground myself in it. I stop seeing the situation for what it *seems* to be and start seeing it for the workout situation I *know* it to be. After that, I can handle it."

The possessions, the vacations, the financial security, and having enough to share are only the outer benefits of Caleb's inner changes. What Caleb is most happy with is his inner state of well-being and feeling free from the inadequacy that tormented his earlier life.

EXERCISE NUMBER ONE

Start Seeing Challenges as Workout Situations

Memorize the following statement and write it down on several pieces of paper:

The events that occur in my life are workout situations. They are there for my benefit so I can become strong and gain wisdom and information by working my way through those situations.

Carry that message with you, tape it on your mirror, on the ceiling over your bed, on the dashboard of your car, on your desk at work, on your schoolbooks if you're a student, on the breakfast table, and on objects in other places where you spend time.

Bring this thought to mind in your day-to-day affairs. Live it. Begin to respond to events with that truth in mind. This is an exceptionally powerful concept. When you utilize this one concept, and use it fully, it will improve the quality of your life in many ways that will amaze and delight you.

EXERCISE NUMBER TWO

Be Aware of Events as Mirrors

During an entire day, see yourself "as if from a distance" and keep in control. That means that in the morning when you become aware that you're awake, even if your eyes are still closed, look at your mental state and take charge of it. Realize that it's a "just right" day for you, regardless of what you're going to do that day. You can say, "This is *my* day!" Hold on to that thought all day.

Keep aware of your thoughts while you're brushing your teeth, getting dressed, and during your other daily routines. See your thoughts as mirrors. Remember: what you do, how you do it, and how you react to events are all indications of "Who You Are." As you are going through a situation, remember that you are going to be looking at it later on in the day to see how you handled it—to see if you were living up to the high standards you expect from yourself.

During the day, look at everything you do as if you were looking in a mirror. Naturally bring out your best abilities. Radiate good will, cheerfulness, and well-being in your contact with people. See them as mirrors, and act in a way that will cause them to reflect the person you want to be.

Keep aware during stressful events that they are simply workout situations. Keep aware of what you are feeling, how you are acting, and what you are thinking.

You may become very concerned about a particular event, get caught up in it and forget to be aware that you are to be "looking at yourself." If that happens, go back over the event afterwards. Mentally view yourself, see how you acted, how you felt, what you thought. Each event is a mirror. Use it to become aware of "Who You Are," and act in such a manner that the "Who You Are" that is reflected in that mirror (event) is who you want to be.

Your goal for this exercise is to spend most of one day being aware of yourself and "Who You Are" and seeing the events of your day as workout situations. If you fail to spend most of one day in that state of awareness, do it for another day. You may consider this exercise complete *only* when you have spent most of one entire day being aware. Keeping aware is tough work, as you will discover, but you can do it. As you work with the program in this book, continue to be aware. By doing this, you will bring about the change you want to see. This exercise is very powerful and will bring about results that will cause you to wonder if it's really you who is doing it.

EXERCISE NUMBER THREE

Completing a Small Task

Pay extra-close attention to this exercise. Choose a small task that needs to be done, something you've been putting off. Choose a simple task that you can accomplish in a relatively short period of time. It might be putting your desk or closet in order, patching up a hurt friendship, straightening out a misunderstanding, or improving a situation. The main part of this exercise is to complete the task *to your complete satisfaction*. That means you are going to do it really well, as well as you can.

Be thoughtful in choosing your task. If you find that the task involving the desk, closet, hurt friendship, or whatever you chose is a major task rather than a simple one, choose something else for this exercise. One person who worked with this program had recently moved into a new apartment and chose getting the apartment in order as her task. That was too hard because it took her several weeks. Another person chose delivering some clothes to the cleaners on her way to work, but that was too easy. The perfect task for this exercise is right there as part of your life. Read the first paragraph again to get a feel for your task.

Avoid setting a time for when the task should be completed. When planning your task, don't set a specific time for your completion of the task, such as "I will finish my task by tomorrow at 5:30 p.m." If you fail to meet that deadline, you will feel that you have failed irreversibly in completing your goal. The amount of time it takes to accomplish your task is the least important consideration in this exercise.

Focus your attention. As in the beginning of all things, the beginning of your task is of great importance. Focus your attention fully and keep aware that you are fulfilling an exercise that will greatly enhance your ability to have things the way you want them. Completing your task with care will prepare you for all that is to come, which is more than the rest of this program—it's the rest of your life.

Observe your attitude. Finishing the task you choose is an important symbol of completion. The process of doing it is equally important. Do it well and *to your complete satisfaction*. Use your full determination in bringing about its fulfillment. The task you choose is a workout situation, so observe yourself and your attitude as you go through it. Do you work cheerfully or are you cross? Is your attitude in completing the task one of eagerness and anticipation in being on a new path of self-development that leads to what you want? Or are you doing it as just another chore that you must get over and done with? If you finish your task haphazardly or in a sloppy manner, you will not be getting what you should out of this exercise.

Fulfill your task knowing that it is mirroring your every thought and action. Your finished product and your mood in doing your task are an expression of "Who You Are." So accomplish your task in such a manner that you will be proud of "Who You Are."

You may believe that you are already a fairly accomplished person and that performing this small task satisfactorily is well within your capability. Therefore you might be tempted to perform this exercise only passably. Reconsider! When you come to have what you desire in your life, you want to be *completely satisfied*, and this exercise is helping you understand what that means and how that feels. You are getting to know how to bring that about. Complete satisfaction is on its way to becoming a central feature of your life.

When you plan to finish a task to your complete satisfaction, it often takes on a whole new aspect. Simply getting a task done and out of the way may only take a short time. The same task accomplished to your complete satisfaction may take ten times the effort and time.

After I finished writing this book, I did the exercises so I would know what you were going to experience. For this exercise, my task was to put a finish on both sides of a beautiful piece of wood from Africa that I planned on using for a small table top. The wood was circular, about two inches thick, and about twenty inches across. When I began, I thought, "This is just right. A couple of hours and I'll have this finished." However, each time I thought I was finished, I asked myself, "Is this done to my complete satisfaction?" and dozens of times I had to answer no, and I would go back to work.

I worked on my project whenever I had a few hours, and it took nearly a month before I could say I had done it as well as I could do it. As a result, I brought to the next project I undertook a new awareness of how to complete something to my complete satisfaction. You will, too, if you pick the right task. My new awareness is still with me today whenever I undertake to accomplish something. I never leave it until I've done it as well as I can and *to my complete satisfaction*.

See any obstacles as opportunities. This exercise and the others in this book are helping you build the strengths that, when fully developed, will enable you to reach every goal. If events occur that get in the way of accomplishing your goal, that's perfect. See them as perfect opportunities to focus your attention more strongly. By overcoming the obstacles, you will build the strengths you need for other and greater accomplishments. The steps you need to take to get to the next level of your development are part of the framework of your life. They are there now, and they are perfectly suited to you. That's why they are there. There are no coincidences.

Write about the task. After you have chosen your task, turn to page 48 and under the heading "My Task" write down your task.

Next, write anything you want in describing your task—for example, how you feel about it or why you have previously put off doing it, even if it's just that you haven't gotten around to it.

During and after the fulfillment of your task, write any comments about yourself that you observed while performing the task and describe any new awareness you develop. After you have completed your task, write the date of completion.

My Task:

Date completed: ______________________________

EXERCISE NUMBER FOUR

Learning to Be Happy—
Pleasure Exercise #2

Enjoy another half hour of pleasure. Begin by saying, *"I, [say your name], give myself permission to enjoy a half hour of pleasure."* The second step is to decide what your pleasure exercise will be. The third step is to turn to the page at the end of this chapter headed "Pleasure Exercise #2" and write down your choice of what to do. Then treat yourself to your half hour of pleasure. Complete this exercise in any way you see fit, but make certain it is a full half hour of pleasure. If it is marred in any way, start over or choose another pleasure exercise.

Complete the exercises in this chapter before going on to chapter 4.

Pleasure Exercise #2:

Date completed: ______________________________

4

THE PERFECT YOU

Why should you look for treasure abroad?
Within yourself you have a bright pearl!
—Pao-chih

IMAGINE THE EARTH—with all of its mountains, oceans, and plains, its forests, jungles, and deserts—condensing, becoming smaller, first to half its size, then to a quarter of its size, and then to the size of North America. The Earth in its smaller size still weighs as much as it did originally, but now it is compacted. As the Earth compacts, it generates enormous energy in the form of heat and light. It glows hotter and hotter, brighter and brighter.

Now imagine the Earth with its remaining, already compacted mass squeezing down to the size of a ball one hundred feet in diameter. Think how dense it would be, how heavy. A teaspoonful of this compacted Earth would weigh trillions of tons. Imagine the Earth condensing still further to the size of a tiny grain of sand. As it condenses, it generates incredible heat. It glows and radiates like a tiny sun, but far more brilliantly. Imagine this tiny grain that is the entire

Earth continuing to shrink until suddenly it ceases to have physical substance at all and births into another dimension, a dimension that lacks form but is still "held together" by a force—a force of desire to be held together. We'll call it "consciousness."

This consciousness is aware of itself, a perfect "Itself." For this awareness to experience all that is to be experienced on the physical plane, it needs a physical body. The opportunity for this occurs when the male sperm joins with the female egg and the new "being" begins to attract cells to itself.

What you have just read in this chapter is an idea of what consciousness might be like, but however consciousness comes about, know that you are not just a body; you are an awareness, a consciousness, a vast collection of energy—able to create, to move, to think, and to do, even to destroy or kill. I don't mean kill in the total sense of the word, because that part was left out when the Universe was formed. You can't "kill" energy or consciousness; you can only change its form, as when you burn a stick of wood, changing it into heat energy.

As far as we can tell, we are the only ones in the Universe who have our particular kind of life or consciousness. Our scientists haven't found evidence of life anywhere in the Universe except right here on Planet Earth. From what you have read in earlier chapters, you know that I believe that life exists in everything—that life is energy in all its various forms and that energy is conscious. I also said that many people, particularly scientists, believe that life only exists within a biological form, and so for them much of the Universe is lifeless. For me, the entire Universe is blazingly alive, vibrantly alive, teeming with life. Life is all there is; there is nothing that is not life. We are spiritual beings having this incredible human experience. We have been gifted with this fantastic, wondrous, splendid, dazzling, magnificent, miraculous consciousness, this awe-inspiring being-ness. It's my favorite thing.

Because your awareness of yourself as this wondrous being is absent at birth, and because you learn through trial and error, you have come to believe that you sometimes do things in the wrong way—that you are less than perfect. However, the truth is, to say it in a comical way, you are perfectly perfect. Your body and brain go through a training period. You learn how to walk, run, throw a ball, speak, sit, stand, write, read, and move. We learn many lessons—some well, others poorly. But you are *always* a perfect being.

The idea that people are less than perfect has given rise to the saying "Well, I'm only human," meaning we are lowly humans who make mistakes. Only human? That's a huge put-down. How about wonderfully human, fabulously human, stupendously human, miraculously human, fantastically human, phenomenally human, *gloriously* human? Did you learn from your mistake? Of course you did. But most of the time, people emphasize your "mistake" rather than the lesson you got out of it. So what you usually heard was "*You're* wrong," as though there was something wrong with *you*. They didn't say, "That was a mistake, but you are a perfect being learning to use your body and brain, which is done by practicing. And in practicing, you'll make what *seem* to be mistakes, and you may *seem* to fail, but you are *always* a perfect spiritual being."

You might feel that you are less than completely well spoken, less than completely capable, less than completely good looking, or that you lack other qualities you think are desirable. However, you are still a perfect being. You may have been born with only one ear, in which case you are a perfect one-eared being.

Here's an analogy that will help you understand this concept further. Electricity is a form of perfect energy, but sometimes it operates through a faulty machine. Although it appears to be working improperly, the electricity still retains its perfectness, its essentially pure nature and energy form. Likewise, you, as a perfect, radiant being, are operating through a physical body that is less than 100 percent efficient, less than 100 percent trained. You may appear to be working improperly when you make a mistake, become ill, have a physical impairment, or otherwise seem to fail. But you *are* a perfect being.

It's especially difficult to see yourself as a perfect being if you have a physical ailment such as a cancer that is overtaking your body, but you must realize that you are not completely defined by your physical body. Your physical self is the substance your conscious-being self collected to gain physical experience. Any thought that you are completely defined by your physical self is false. You are a perfect spiritual being. Get used to that idea.

WHO YOU THINK YOU ARE

The moment your brain became functional, you began to build an image of who and what you believed yourself to be. All the events of your life have helped to create the image of "Who You Think You Are." Perhaps a parent told you from the time you were very young, "You're wonderful, and I love you." Those words will remain in your memory, supplying you with that information no matter what else happens to you. Each time someone is critical of you, the words of your parent will still be there: "You're wonderful, and I love you." It is a fortunate child who receives that kind of positive image-building.

On the other hand, you may have had experiences that reinforced the opposite belief. Perhaps when you were three years old, you were given a new toy that you broke shortly after receiving it, and the parent who gave you the gift exclaimed, "You're so clumsy!" That criticism may have hurt you. Maybe you thought about it a lot. Perhaps the following week you bumped into a vase and knocked it over and it broke. Perhaps someone saw the incident and said, "Watch what you're doing. You're so clumsy!" Afterwards, when you dropped something or hurt yourself, you may have thought, "I'm clumsy." Although many years have passed and you've forgotten the original incidents, those words are there, feeding you from a subconscious level, saying, "I'm clumsy."

Your parents were not the only ones who contributed to your self-image. Children, siblings, friends, and other adults participated in your image-building. Imagine for a moment that when you were in the second grade, you were attracted to the child with the soft brown eyes. Imagine that you went over to the child and very timidly said, "Would you like to eat your lunch with me?" And the child replied, "What! Eat my lunch with a creep like you? I'd rather eat my lunch with a toad!" You crept back to your desk, hoping you were the only one who had heard the remark. The embarrassment and hurt impressed itself upon your mind. You began to form an image of yourself *as seen through the eyes of the person who made the remark*.

It probably took a long time for you to make such an attempt again. Imagine the next time you tried to do the same thing, perhaps years later, and with a different person. You may have said something like, "Ah, well, um, I, ah, was wondering if you would like to, ah, maybe, um, well, you know, eat your lunch with me?" Perhaps the person laughed at you and said jeeringly, "Duh! No thanks!" The image of yourself that you had formed from the first experience influenced the way you acted the second time, which, in turn, helped to create the second harsh response, reinforcing and solidifying your negative self-image. After two such harsh image-forming events, it is doubtful that you would make another attempt for many years. By that time, even if those two events had faded from your memory, the image they created would still feed you from a subconscious level, still influence the way you act, and still be a strong part of "Who You Think You Are."

So, here you are, a perfect, radiant being, operating through a brain that has been programmed with at least some of the limitations I listed in chapter 1 or concepts like "You'd better do well in school, honey, because you're never going to make it on your looks." "You'll never amount to anything." "You're a failure, just like your father/mother was." "It's your fault that your brother/sister/friend hurt himself/herself." "You never do anything right." "You're such a loser." The radiant being you truly are is always complete and fully present, but its radiance has been clouded, its brilliance dulled. The radiant being you *truly* are has become covered over with layers of false images, misconceptions, and flaws that you have come to accept as the real you. After a while, the outer covering—the seemingly real you—seems to be the *only* you. Fortunately, you can correct that.

THE POWER OF YOUR IMAGINATION

To give your perfect being the freedom to express itself clearly, you must replace the perception in your mind that you are anything less than a perfect, radiant being. Before I show you how, there are some foundational concepts you should understand.

Our minds and our imaginations are powerful tools. Research has shown that our bodies and minds react to an imagined experience in much the same way that they do to an actual experience. When researchers from Harvard University tested subjects in a brain scanner, they found that seeing a picture of a tree and imagining a tree activated the same parts of the brain.[1] One interesting study showed that people who just imagined doing a certain physical exercise, without doing it physically, still increased their muscular strength.[2]

You don't need to be a scientist to know how powerful your imagination is. I'm sure you've experienced your mouth watering when you're hungry or when you think about certain foods. When you imagine a piece of chalk making a squeaky sound on a blackboard, you get a shiver up your back. When you close your eyes and imagine yourself walking on a tightrope across a deep canyon, you might experience some of the frightening sensations that you would experience by actually doing it. When you go through a heavily impressive experience, you can remember it years later and experience some of the same feelings and emotions that were originally present. Men and women feel a sexual response when thinking of making love.

Your imagination can transform you, and it is especially powerful when you are in the relaxed state known as the alpha state. While you're awake and active, when you're going about your daily activities and are thinking, problem solving, and processing information, your brain ordinarily functions at around thirteen to thirty cycles per second. That's called the beta level. Sleep, on the other hand, occurs when your brain is functioning at about eight cycles per second and lower.

As you lie down to prepare for sleep, your breathing slows, your heartbeat slows, and, consequently, your brain cycles begin to slow. At that point, you are in the alpha state, where your brain is functioning at around eight to twelve cycles per second. You are also at the alpha level when you are just waking up and when, during the day, you are in a relaxed but aware state of consciousness. At the alpha level, you are calm and at ease and you can experience a marvelous flow of thoughts, ideas, and creativity. You are also more receptive to suggestions.

At the alpha level, your imagination acts powerfully on your subconscious mind and therefore your imaginings are powerfully effective in producing the desired result. It is believed that our subconscious mind represents nearly 90 percent of our mental capacity, which is why influencing your subconscious mind produces such powerful effects. This next exercise is highly pleasurable and will strongly influence your subconscious mind, changing forever "Who You Think You Are."

OVERWRITING YOUR OLD SELF-IMAGE

You are now going to journey to the alpha level, where you will use your imagination to create an image of yourself that will overwrite the image you currently hold in your subconscious mind of "Who You Think You Are." Your new image is "Who You Want to Be." The first part of the title of this book is "Be Who You Want." This exercise plays a major part in bringing that about. Once that is achieved, the second part of the title, "Have What You Want," will naturally come about as a result of having achieved the first part.

Without being aware of it, you have struggled most of your life to live as your perfect self, trying to overcome the negative effects of the "assumed" image that was impressed on your mind by parents, teachers, friends, and even yourself as you began to believe the negative things you were told about yourself. You are going to end that struggle now by creating a new image, a perfect image, that will overwrite your old image. It's the same as rerecording over a videotape or a CD.

When you journey to the alpha level in the meditation that follows, you will see that *everything* is just the way you want it to be and *only* as you imagine it to be. Once there, you will meet your subconscious "perfect image" and experience that image with your conscious mind. When your conscious mind experiences your subconscious perfect image, it will be powerfully influenced by the experience. Through repetition, you will begin to act as your perfect image would act. You will begin to act as if your perfect image is the only image you have of "Who You Are," which will actually be true.

Acting as your perfect image will naturally bring about new results, results different from the results your old, flawed image produced. You will see yourself the way you were meant to be, as you *already* exist on the subconscious, perfect-image level.

That means you will see all of yourself as perfect—your physical self, your career self, your social self, your student self, and all the other selves that make up you. You will saturate the part of your mind that is your everyday consciousness with subconscious images of your perfect being. You are going to *overwrite* the flawed image you hold of yourself with a wonderful, bright new image that is the *real* you. As you continue to expose your conscious mind to your subconscious perfect image, you will feel immensely better about yourself, you will act from the deep level of your subconscious perfect image, and you will produce results consistent with your perfect image. This is one of the most effective ways to become who you want. Once you have achieved that, can you imagine that your perfect image will bring you what you want as well? Of course it will!

Give yourself up to this exercise. Allow your mind to roam freely in this perfect world of your imagination. Don't hold back. Turn off phones and the TV and guard against interruptions.

Begin by seeing you as you would *like* to look. If you would like to be slimmer or have longer hair or be in top physical condition, in your imagination see yourself that way. If you would like to be more courageous, more daring, more outgoing, more effective in your life, more popular, more affluent, and less afraid, less out of shape, less timid, less unimaginative, well, this is your opportunity to see yourself exactly as you would like to be. As you experience this journey to the alpha level, *allow yourself the luxury of letting go.* Read slowly, and as the words unfold, pause often and let your imagination have full reign. Allow yourself to flow with the words as you read them.

At first, this takes a high degree of concentration because thoughts of the day will intrude into your thinking process. Consciously push those thoughts aside and keep your attention fixed on what you are doing. It helps to have soft music, without any vocals, quietly playing in the background. Flutes are a good choice. If you elect to have music playing, be sure that the recording will last at least as long as your journey, perhaps twenty minutes.

At the alpha level, you will see things in a certain way. *Whatever* way you see them is correct. If, for instance, you are asked in this meditation to imagine golden stairs, whatever kind of stairs you imagine and in whatever shape you imagine them is correct. They can be spiral or straight, round or square. They can rise quickly or slowly. Whatever you see is correct for you. If you are asked to imagine a pond, the pond can be as wide as a street or as wide as a football field. Whatever you see is correct for you. If you're going to have soft music playing, this is the time to start it.

You may think you are conjuring up your perfect image with your imagination. That is not so. You are actually bringing your perfect image forth from the Source of All-That-Is, *where it already exists.* The same is true for the fields, pond, rocks, flowers, waterfall, and other parts of your place of ideal relaxation that you are going to call forth from the Source with your imagination. I capitalize *Source* to help you keep in mind that your Source is the conscious, totally aware Universe. Remember that your subconscious mind does not know the difference between an imagined experience and an experience you have when you are not imagining. Both experiences are real. You are not alone; *the Universe is aware of your quest.* It is aware of what you are now doing. It will assist you.

MEDITATION ON THE PERFECT YOU

To begin this liberating journey, find a comfortable chair, and relax. Slowly expel all the air from your lungs and hold it out for a moment.

Now, ever so slowly, inhale. Slowly, slowly fill your lungs to capacity, and now hold your breath, perhaps for three or four seconds. *Slowly* exhale, mentally repeating the word *relax* three times.

When your lungs are empty of air again, wait quietly for two or three seconds. Follow the words carefully, fully, giving yourself time to feel what's happening. *Feel* the relaxation beginning to take hold. *Feel* yourself slowing down.

Now, slowly inhale, filling your lungs to capacity . . . hold it, and then *slowly* exhale, mentally repeating the word *relax* three times.

Experience what a good feeling it is to be so relaxed. Feel your eyelids relax. Move your head from side to side and feel your neck muscles relax. Take your time . . . allow this feeling to float slowly downward, relaxing your whole body.

As I name each part of your body, momentarily tense the muscles in that area and then relax them. Now, feel your face muscles relax . . . your shoulders . . . take your time with this . . . your chest . . . feel it . . . your back . . . your arms . . . your wrists . . . let the relaxation take hold . . . your hands and fingers . . . your waist . . . your hips and thighs . . . your knees . . . the calves of your legs . . . your ankles . . . your feet and toes. Feel your whole body in its relaxed state. Feel it . . . .

Now, slowly expel all the air from your lungs and hold it out, perhaps for three or four seconds. Now, slowly, slowly inhale, filling your lungs to capacity, and hold it, perhaps for three or four seconds, then slowly exhale, repeating the word *relax* three times.

Read slowly. Now that you have slowed your breathing, you're ready to experience a deeper, more relaxed level of mind. Mentally count backwards from ten to one—one number for each inward breath and one number for each outward breath. With each descending number, feel yourself becoming more and more relaxed as your mental cycles begin to slow and you drift to the level of mind just before sleep.

Ten, inward breath . . . nine, slow outward breath . . . eight, inward breath—one slow breath for each number. Seven, exhale slowly . . . six, inhale—drifting ever downward, drifting, drifting. Five, exhale slowly—like a feather floating softly down, down to the level just before sleep. Four, inhale . . . three, slowly exhale—down and down. Two, inhale . . . then one, a long, slow exhale. Feel how relaxed you are. What a good feeling that is.

You are now at a deeper, more relaxed level of mind, and you are calmer and more peaceful. Use this deep level of mind to go to an even deeper, more relaxed level of mind. Slowly expel all the air from your lungs and hold it out for a moment.

Now, slowly, slowly inhale, filling your lungs with air, and hold it for a moment. Now, slowly exhale, going deeper and deeper to the level of mind just above sleep.

This is the level where all things are exactly as you wish them to be. This is the level of power and imagination, where you are always in complete control.

Now . . . imagine rolling meadows covered with lush green grass. See that. Now, in your mind's eye, see beautiful flowers of many different colors all around. The sun is shining gently. A soft breeze is blowing, moving the grass gently. Watch the grass as it gently bends under the soft breeze. There are big, inviting rocks scattered around. Birds fly about and sing. Butterflies of different colors float gently on the breeze. What a perfect spot this is. Experience what it feels like to be in this lovely meadow, your meadow.

Near the center of the meadow is a pond with trees growing at its edge. Some of their branches hang gracefully down and touch the water. Walk over to the pond and look into the crystal-clear water. See the tiny, colorful fish swim by—friendly fish. See the reeds growing by the side of the pond and a small island in the center.

On the other side of the pond is a waterfall about ten feet high, a magical waterfall whose waters come from the Source of all things. See the water as it plunges over the edge and into the pond. See the sunlight glinting on the water and the rainbow that's created as the spray drifts on the wind.

Walk over to this waterfall and feel the spray. The temperature is just right. Now let your clothing disappear and step under the gentle waterfall. It is exactly the right temperature. Ah, how good that feels.

Mentally, put your hands over your head and turn around. Feel the water as it cascades down over your hands and arms, your head and shoulders, your chest and back—refreshing you, cleansing you, washing away all you wish to be free of. Feel these magical waters as they wash away your tiredness. See the tiredness as dust being washed away, leaving you strong and refreshed, vital and alive.

Feel the magical waters wash away all feelings of resentment and frustration. Allow any feelings you have of resentment and frustration to dissolve and float away from you, released by the waterfall. Allow all guilt and anxiety, all feelings of sinfulness and depression to wash away. See them as dust, washed away by the powerful waters, dissolving and leaving you clean, whole, pure, innocent, virtuous, and free. See if there is anything in your past you wish to be free of. These healing waters will wash away anything you wish to be free of. See these waters wash it all away now, leaving you pure, virtuous, and free.

These magical waters also have the power to heal you of all manner of ailments. Give yourself up to the healing power of this magical waterfall. Feel the healing nature of the water as it washes over you. You can breathe in this water. Breathe in this water now. Feel the water as it courses through your body, purifying every cell, every bone, every organ, causing them to sparkle and glow with health and vitality.

Feel the remarkable water cascading over and through your whole body, exhilarating you, filling you with its power. Feel the waterfall wash away everything you wish to have washed away, leaving you pure and free.

Now take a deep breath through your nose and let it out quickly through your mouth. And now do it again.

Step out from under the waterfall and stand beside the pond. Feel the sun gently warming you, cleansing you, purifying you. Feel its rays shining through you, filling you with its radiance, causing you to glow and shimmer. Feel the wind softly drying you—penetrating through you, healing you, causing you to feel light and free. Now cause yourself to be clothed in a white robe, soft, light, and luxurious.

Next, mentally create a seat for yourself. It can be of any material you like—wood, cloth, even air. For you, it's the most comfortable place in all the world. Settle yourself into the seat now and relax. Feel how absolutely comfortable that is—how perfect. See the blue sky, the occasional white puffy cloud, the birds flying by. Everything here is exactly as you wish it to be. Here, you are in complete control. This is your perfect place of ideal relaxation and peace. It is more uniquely your own than anything else on Earth. You have called this place forth from the Source of all that exists and it is *truly* yours. Here, you get to decide the way everything is. Here, you are *completely* in charge.

Now, call forth the image of your perfect being by seeing yourself exactly as you would like to be. See your perfect image standing, facing you, about ten feet away, clothed in a white robe, the same as yours. See everything you could ever want to be. See how natural you look. Look at your hair—see what color it is, what length it is. See your skin and notice the texture of it. Have your perfect image raise its hands over its head and turn about. Look closely at the back of your image. Have your image continue turning until it faces you again. How graceful. How full of poise.

Get up from your seat and walk over to your perfect image. Look into the eyes of your perfect image. See how clear they are. Smile at your perfect image and see your perfect image smiling back at you. Your perfect image knows *everything* there is to know about you *and loves you completely*.

Hold out your right arms toward each other and clasp wrists. Feel the energy and power leaving your perfect image and passing to you. Feel yourself glowing. See your perfect image glowing.

Release wrists and see your perfect image turning around and facing away from you. Walk closer to your perfect image and step right into it, merging with it.

Now, as your perfect image, put your hands over your head and turn around. See how wonderful that feels. How graceful. Dance about a little. How light and strong! Walk over to your most comfortable seat and rest a moment *as your perfect image*. What a good feeling. How relaxed, how much in control you are. *This is the real you.*

Repeat the following sentences in a whisper:

> *From this moment forward, I am in control of every situation. I will always know the exact right words to speak. I will always know the exact right action to take, and this is so. I will now obtain vibrant good health. I will have the possessions I want. I now have power, and this is so. I will have peace and harmony in my life. I will have wonderful love and abundance, and this is so. I claim all these things for my own from this time forward.*

Take a few minutes or more to create for yourself, in your imagination, any situation or possession you desire. Close your eyes and see it in great detail. Now that you have finally reached your perfect place, enjoy it. Do this now, before you continue reading the next paragraph. Know that whatever beneficial thing you will envision is even now on its way to you, and this is so.

Now that you have envisioned what you want, it is time to ascend to your new life. Across from the pond are ten golden stairs that lead up to a new everyday consciousness. See the sun as it sparkles on the stairs. See how they shine. As your perfect image, walk over to those stairs now.

Soon, you will ascend these stairs with all the power, love, and peace you have visualized for yourself here in this perfect place of power and ideal relaxation. You will ascend these stairs, leaving behind all the things that were washed away by the waterfall and that dissolved into nothingness. You are free. You are pure. You are whole. You are virtuous. You are powerful. Hold that image of yourself in your mind.

Slowly climb these golden stairs now, one step for each inward breath and one step for each outward breath. One, inhale . . . two, exhale . . . three . . . four.

Pause, turn around, and look over this paradise you have created for yourself. See the pond and the trees and the flowers. See the waterfall and the blue sky. There is a magnificent rainbow arching from one side to the other. See how it glows and shimmers.

Here, in this perfect place, everything is exactly the way you wish it to be. You may return here at any time. Just by desiring to be here, you will be here instantly. Here you may refresh yourself in the waterfall, washing away fatigue and frustration and anything else you wish to be free of. You may breathe in and drink the healing waters and fill yourself with virtue, power, and healing. You may rest in your seat and call forth from the Source the things you desire. You can receive ideas and inspiration, and you can create possessions or situations you want for yourself. In this ideal place, you can have your perfect image appear at any time so that you can once again look lovingly at each other, and you can see how you have grown more like your perfect image every time you return.

Now, as your perfect image, continue climbing the stairs to your everyday consciousness, one breath for every step. Five, inhale. Six—climb with power and virtue and love. Seven—feel refreshed. Eight—feel very calm and peaceful. Nine—feel more alert. Ten—feel completely rested, as if you have slept a whole night soundly and well.

You are now here, as your perfect image. Your perfect image does not lie, has no bad habits, is all-powerful, is completely virtuous, is free to come and go as you choose, is at one with All-That-Is, and loves you completely. Trust it to know what to do in every situation. Trust it to know how to care for you and those in your care. Trust it.

The journey you have just taken can greatly support you in becoming who you want to be and in bringing about what you want to have. When you bathe your conscious mind with the image of your perfect being, your conscious mind becomes saturated with the assets, virtues, and powers of your perfect image. As you continue with this exercise, you will begin to act from the level of your perfect image and, consequently, you will create results compatible with your perfect image. That's when you'll smile . . . a lot.

YOU CREATE YOUR REALITY

Your perfect image is one with eternity. As the weeks pass and you become familiar with your perfect image, you will naturally and effortlessly begin to act as your perfect image. When you're talking to another person, doing a chore, or are engaged in other activities, feel yourself *being* your perfect image and allow yourself to be that way. Trust your perfect image. By being "Who You Are," you create your reality moment by moment. The Universe always responds to you as you are being at every moment.

"Who You Think You Are" will change as you follow this program. Let that happen. Act as the extra-special person you meet in your imagination, because on that level you *are* that person. By experiencing your perfect image, you will bring that being to the surface of your life and everything will be different for you—far better, far brighter, far easier, far more possible.

Drop all aspects of "you" that are not part of your perfect image, aspects like fear, smoking, using alcohol or drugs, swearing, weakness, lying, meanness, stinginess, and all limitations that are obstacles to achieving your goals. "Who You Think You Are" is now going through the same process a caterpillar goes through to become a butterfly. Let the process happen *and fly*.

The image of "Who You Think You Are" has been around since the day you were born. Your "perfect" image has been around since the dawn of time. It is as bright, fresh, vital, alive, and powerful as the first brilliant day of the Universe. It is *all-powerful*. It is you.

EXERCISE NUMBER ONE

Taking the Journey

It's essential that you keep in touch with the image of your perfect being. Take the alpha-level journey once a day for thirty days. Then let one week pass before beginning again. Repeat that schedule for six months, taking the journey once a day for thirty days and then letting one week pass without doing it. *Mark your calendar now*. If you want to continue to take the alpha-level journey after six months, you may do so.

In the Power Workshops I conducted, the participants sat with their eyes closed while soft music played in the background and my voice guided them on their journey to the alpha level. If you would like to have the experience of being guided on your meditation, visit www.PowerPressPublishing.com to order the CD that will guide you on your journey.

EXERCISE NUMBER TWO

Imagining Your Perfect Day

For the next three nights, after you are in bed, lie quietly and imagine yourself going through your day *as* your perfect image. Spend at least three minutes doing this exercise. You may use more time if you wish. See yourself reacting to events, talking with people, and fulfilling your goals as your perfect image. See your goals being achieved. This exercise is best done just after you complete exercise #1 above.

The pleasurable exercises you are doing will powerfully influence your subconscious mind. As you sleep, your subconscious mind is fully awake and fully functioning, creating "Who You Think You Are," who is rapidly becoming "Who You Are." You will quickly see the results of these powerful exercises as you go through your day. You will be more alert, more capable, more in charge, and more aware, producing results that are more in line with what you want. I'm excited for you!

EXERCISE NUMBER THREE

Learning to Be Happy—Pleasure Exercise #3

Enjoy another half hour of pleasure. Begin by saying, *"I, [say your name], give myself permission to enjoy a half hour of pleasure."* The second step is to decide what your pleasure exercise will be. The third step is to turn to the page at the end of this chapter headed "Pleasure Exercise #3" and write down your choice of what to do. Then treat yourself to your half hour of pleasure.

Fulfill this exercise outdoors. Make this half hour extra-special. Pamper yourself. Treat yourself as a perfect being. At the end of the half hour, if you find that it has been less than pleasurable, start over or choose another pleasure exercise. Do this exercise as the perfect being you are. Halfway measures are not acceptable. You deserve a full half hour of absolute pleasure. Make sure you get it.

When you have completed your pleasure exercise, write the date and a brief summary of what happened, how you felt, and any other special thing you care to write about under the heading "Pleasure Exercise #3." Be thoughtful in what you write so that you can later benefit from your experience.

When you have fulfilled the first session of Exercise Number One, you may consider it complete for the purpose of moving ahead to chapter 5. Fully complete Exercises Two and Three of this chapter before moving ahead to the next chapter. As before, do not read ahead until you have fulfilled these exercises.

Pleasure Exercise #3:

Date completed: ______________________________

5

THE WORLD OF PERFECT

The world is full of magical things patiently waiting for our wits to grow sharper.
—Bertrand Russell

IN 1983, I WENT FOR THE FIRST TIME to the Hawaiian island of Kauai, the most northerly and the oldest of the Hawaiian Island chain. Kauai is known as the "Garden Isle" because it is lush and tropical—an exquisite jewel. At its center is Mount Waialiali, one of the wettest spots on earth. It rains about 450 inches a year. My fun-loving friend Thomas, who lived on the island, was my guide to the various sites of tropical splendor. Every time we came to a new place, he would laugh and say, "The next one's better!" Finally, we came to a high cliff and looked over the edge, straight down into the Pacific Ocean.

He grinned and said, "I saved the best one for last."

Everything I saw was a shimmering, glistening, spectacular panorama of beauty. "Thomas, this is exquisite!" I exclaimed.

We walked a short distance to a new vantage point that overlooked a small valley with a winding stream that gurgled and laughed and sparkled on its way to the ocean. In the valley was a small farm area with healthy, vibrant vegetables and a garden adorned with bright flowers that nodded their heads in every direction. During our tour of the garden, Tom said, "This is nice, but the best part is further down, where the land meets the ocean."

It was hard to believe there could be something better than what I had just seen. We walked along a path that followed the stream and soon came to an area where the trail meandered around the side of a hill, revealing the mouth of the stream. The small cliff over which the stream plunged was crescent shaped and the water looked like melted glass as it fell fifteen feet into the tidal pools below. In the tidal pools swam fish of every description. Slightly to the north was a peninsula, perhaps a hundred yards long, and it was split in half to form a crevice that ran from its tip back to the cliff, where it widened into an underground cave. The waves plunged into the crevice and ran its entire length till they disappeared under the cliff wall and then smashed into the back of the cave with a pound and a roar that shook the earth.

Further out and slightly to the south was a jut of rocks that pushed their way into the ocean about a hundred and fifty feet. The U-shaped lagoon created by these two arms of land seemed alive as the shimmering aquamarine water rose and fell with the waves. It was one of the most beautiful places I'd ever seen.

"This is paradise!" I exclaimed.

"This little farm belongs to me, Chris, and I want you to come here and visit anytime you like."

It was as if St. Peter had just opened the pearly gates! I planned my first visit for the very next day.

This opportunity fit in perfectly with a plan I had made to experience a small portion of a vision quest, an Indian ritual I had studied in an exceptional book called *Seven Arrows* by Hyemeyohsts Storm. Storm is an elder Indian who writes from the heart and teaches us the ancient Indian lore through Medicine Wheel stories told around the campfires of the Indian nations. Indians use the vision quest ritual to reach states of heightened awareness, to discover their true Indian names (mine is Sun Eagle), to find their missions in life, and to receive information of a spiritual nature to help them fulfill those missions. Ordinarily, at the start of a vision quest one goes alone into the wilderness naked or dressed only in a loincloth and equipped with a knife or spear. After several days, the lack of food and shelter combine to bring about a state of heightened awareness.

To naturally reach such a state is one of the great experiences life has to offer, and I have sought and found those experiences in many ways. Prior to that day on Kauai, I had been mentally and physically preparing myself for months for this vision quest with a seven-day water fast, meditation, breathing exercises, and envisioning what I hoped for from my vision quest. My state of awareness was already quite keen.

THE ONLY POSSIBILITY

The next morning, I set out equipped with a seven-foot spear for underwater spearfishing, a fishhook and line, a knife, and high hopes. The day was magnificent. The sun shimmered on the ocean, the waves were calm, and the breeze gentle.

I was alone as I made my way down to the tidal pools, took off all my clothing, and, picking up my spear, began the walk that would take me to the tip of the jut of rocks. Climbing naked from rock to rock with my spear as I made my way to the tip of the finger of rocks made me feel very primitive. It took me about ten minutes to reach the tip. From where I was standing, I could see a considerable distance in every direction. From the mountains at the center of the island to the ocean at my back, it seemed as if I was the only person on the island. Visually, there was a complete absence of people, ships, roads, houses, and cars. The only sign that a human had ever lived on the island was an old lean-to off in the distance that had been built on the side of a hill, barely visible through the trees.

I was filled with energy and excitement. My body felt taut, my stomach muscles flat and hard, my thighs and legs powerful. I felt light and springy. My shoulders and chest swelled with power and my eyes saw clearly. The light was superb and the air felt sharp and alive. The ocean breathed gently against the shore. My bare feet, used to shoes and sidewalks, felt a strong awareness of the rock I stood on. A sound came from deep in my throat, drawn by the great primal force of All-That-Is. My body tensed as exhilaration filled me.

Because of my nakedness, I felt very exposed out there on the end of the rocks but unusually alive and excited. I began deep breathing and focused my attention on being a part of it all. I tensed the muscles of my body. I sensed the air moving the hair on my arms and legs, I saw the brilliance of the sun as it flashed on the water, I felt the fine spray from the ocean as the waves broke, and my being responded with an air of urgency—with an "opening," as when the sun's rays fall on a flower.

I knew from reading *Seven Arrows* how to proceed. The four directions each held a gift for me, and I was about to begin the ritual to receive those gifts. Grasping my spear in both hands and raising it above my head, I faced north. My nostrils flared and I cried aloud, "I salute you, great direction of the North, and receive your gift of wisdom!"

It was a strange sensation to be standing there, naked, with a spear raised above my head, shouting into the wind. It felt powerful, unusual, awesome, and a little embarrassing all at the same time. I experienced a rush of adrenalin and my mind seemed to clear even further. My vision sharpened and my other senses intensified. I felt vital and aware in a way I had rarely experienced, and then only at other times of heightened awareness. I turned a quarter turn to the right and again raised my voice and shouted over the ocean:

"I salute you, great direction of the East, and receive your gift of illumination!"

My body tingled. I had goose bumps on my chest, arms, and legs. A surge of power rushed through me. The spear itself felt alive, as if I were holding some great antenna. I turned again and shouted:

"I salute you, great direction of the South, and receive your gifts of trust and innocence!"

All-That-Is responded. Waves crashed, the wind picked up sharply, the forces around me intensified. It was as if the Universe heard me and was responding. I turned a quarter turn for the last time and my voice flew over the land:

"I salute you, great direction of the West, and receive your gift of inward looking!"

I remained standing with my spear raised as a rush of excitement made my heart pound. At times like these, the veils that cover my inner vision fall away, and there, in my mind's eye, is a truth that for years I've been searching for. It's as if I were looking at a page of dots, some darker than others, knowing that they form a picture but failing to see it. Then one day, the picture I've been searching for leaps out at me in sharp clarity and I wonder how I could have ever failed to see it. And once seen, it's impossible to see anything else.

So it was for me on that crystal-clear morning at the tip of the rock jetty in the South Pacific. My nakedness, the strangeness of the ritual I had performed, the vastness around me, the aloneness, the months of mental and physical preparation, my fasting, and my previous times of heightened awareness, all caused the concepts I had so long sought for to form in my mind's eye. I realized then that all I had experienced up to that point in my life—the ordeals, the barriers, and the impediments, all of which I had seen as obstacles, as well as the joys, the exhilarations, and the achievements—were but preparation for that moment and what was to follow.

The wind was blowing my hair, the sun was warming me, the exhilaration was carrying me, carrying my thoughts to places loftier than I had ever experienced. All feelings of strangeness and exposure were gone. I felt relaxed and natural—at home in my Universe. And more than that, I felt my oneness with the Universe. I experienced security and protection, as if there was no separation. The realizations of the way things are, and can be, formed in my mind one after the other:

> *I live in a Universe where the law of cause and effect is absolute. Every action produces a reaction, and the reaction is in exact accord with the action that caused it.*

I am a primary cause. I produce effects that are in perfect accord with how I am being at every moment.

I am the center of my personal Universe. I am the command post sending and receiving everything.

When an event occurs, it is perfect—it is also the only possibility.

Every event that occurs provides me with the greatest possible benefit because it is the Universe that is causing the events and I am the Universe, a part of it.

All things are possible for those who believe that all things are possible.

I am a perfect being—everyone else is too.

You can see from reading this story where and how my philosophy of life took a great leap forward.

A PERFECT AND NECESSARY "NOW"

I walked back to the tidal pools and looked for a long time into the water, thinking of the wonder-filled concepts that had now crystallized in my thoughts. They had been forming for many years, and now that their certainty was upon me, I felt grateful. I was happy and content in a special way. I was happy in the knowledge that I lived in a perfect Universe and that I was as much a part of it as the great galaxies that wheel in space, our sun and moon, the mountains and trees, and the earth itself.

I thought, "I am here, at this wondrous moment in time called 'now,' which is the only moment anyone can experience—for everything else is either a memory (the past) or imagination (the future)—and I am gifted with these wonderful concepts, and I know how to use them!"

I sat and thought about what I had experienced, and then felt hunger pangs begin. I decided to see if I could catch a fish. I rigged a fishing line with a hook and tied a stone to the end of a string for a weight. I pried some bait off the rocks with my knife, then whirled the string around my head, preparing to cast it into the ocean. As I loosed the string, the hook lodged in my finger and the stone shot forward, pulling the hook sharply into my flesh. Blood spurted out. Pain shot up my arm. I looked at the hook sunk into my finger and I spoke aloud my instant reaction: *"Perfect!"*

Here's what I was thinking: "Since everything that happens to me can only be in my best interest, and is therefore the best possible event, everything concerning this 'accident' has to be perfect! At that spot in my finger there must be an acupuncture point that needed piercing." This may sound ridiculous to you, but I laughed aloud, feeling another surge of energy sweep through me. The new concepts were already working! Look what they had just done for me. I had taken a nasty event and turned it into something that increased my awareness and exhilaration. There I was with a fishhook sunk into my finger, feeling good about it! Of course it hurt, *a lot*, but it only seemed to emphasize my newfound information.

The fishhook in my finger symbolized my passage from a world where pain, caused by an isolated, seemingly unlucky event, could put an end to the pleasure of a moment, into a world filled with an endless variety of experiences whose temporary and sometimes unpleasant effects were all united in a single purpose: *a perfect and necessary now that was for my complete benefit.* I realized that my vision quest was continuing to pay dividends, even more than I had hoped for.

I reached out and took hold of the shank of the fish hook, pushed it through, and pulled it out. That really hurt and my finger bled a lot, but my appreciation of the moment was not dimmed in the slightest. All I could do was rejoice in my good fortune. I rinsed my finger in the ocean, wrapped a piece of seaweed around it, and sat down to think about the events of my life that had led me to this moment.

I recalled a time when I was in Naples, Florida, on the Gulf of Mexico. The sunsets are spectacular, and one day as I came to the gulf I was treated to an unusually brilliant blaze of color. Clouds were towering thousands of feet in the sky, looking like muzzle blasts from cannons. The sun had splashed their edges with intense reds, oranges, and yellows, highly accented by white and silver. Streaks of light had broken through parts of the clouds and painted the ocean, sending brilliant sparkles of light in every direction. I remember thinking, "This is a perfect sunset!" A day or two later, I came again and saw yet another spectacular light-and-cloud show and I realized that it, too, was a perfect sunset. I said to myself, "They're all perfect!" And, of course, every sunset that ever was and ever will be is a perfect sunset. Some are more spectacular than others, some are just gray, leaden skies, but all are perfect.

A year after that, I was filming on the Pacific Coast in Big Sur, California, at the top of Pfeiffer Rock. I was operating the camera and had just moved the focus of the lens from the face of the actor down to the ocean about seventy feet below. A big wave was building five hundred yards offshore. I let the camera run as the wave built and grew, and built some more. The face of the wave looked to be about twenty-five feet high. Spindrift was being blown from the top of the wave, creating shimmering rainbows in the air as the wall of water rolled in toward shore.

Finally, the wave crashed with a great resounding roar against the rocks, rocketing spumes of water high in the air. "Perfect!" I thought to myself. I looked out to the ocean and there appeared another wave, just as beautiful, just as big, just as spectacular. "Of course," I thought, "just as perfect. All the waves that ever were and ever will be are perfect."

With that recollection in mind, I dove into the ocean with my spear and came out with a small fish that had been dozing on a rock about six feet down. I filleted the fish and felt, as I consumed it raw, that I had never eaten anything as tasty or as full of vital energy.

HARMONIZING YOURSELF WITH REALITY

The pain in my finger soon subsided and I spent the rest of the day swimming, sunning, and feeling as good as I had ever felt. Late that night, at Hale Moana ("House by the Sea"), where I was staying on Kauai, I wrote the following: "The absolute test to determine if something is perfect is: *if it happened—it is*. The degree to which you can align yourself with that thought is the same degree to which you will have aligned yourself with your Universe. By giving your total agreement to what has happened at every point in time, you have harmonized yourself with reality." I felt really good writing that because I knew it was true.

What is simply "is." You can't reverse time and cause an event to undo itself. All you can do, without exception, is to react to it by liking it or disliking it. The events that have caused your feelings are beyond your power to alter, even a little bit. What you can change are your feelings.

If you feel you have been a victim or have had bad luck or have made a mistake or have been ill-used, you can curse your luck, become angry, or feel frustrated. That's one option. The other option is to look at what happened as being perfect. Then you will feel better in viewing the events of your life, even accidents and apparent tragedies. You will be able to go forward, in step with your Universe. You will come to know that when a seeming mishap occurs, it has a purpose and you'll soon come to know what that is. You will see that what happened is a contribution to the continuing stream of life, and a perfect contribution. You will gain the special vision that it takes to see perfection in all the events of your life.

When you are angry over an event, your attention is focused on the object of your anger. The Universe, however, continues to unfold in all its wondrousness. You are still stuck in the moment when the event took place, anchored there by your anger, missing out on what could be the most important moments of your life.

No matter what happens, your job is to continually nod your head in agreement, validating everything that your Universe is bringing to you as "just right events." It's difficult at first, so don't start on a major event, like an earthquake that has killed thousands. Start with something simple and learn to see the perfection in it. Gradually, you will be able to take on ever-greater events until you have at last arrived at the perfection of the Universe in all events.

Have you ever seen an imperfect wave? An imperfect cloud? An imperfect mountain? Since these are all perfect, and easily seen as such, the next step is easy. See every moment in time as perfect—and more than just the moment itself. See what happens in that moment as perfect as well. *To agree with what happens, to endorse it as perfect, is to be in absolute harmony with the cause of everything.*

If you believe in a higher power that is causing things to happen, then by seeing everything that happens as perfect, you have tuned yourself totally to the higher power that you believe is causing it. You have validated your higher power as perfect and put yourself on its side. It doesn't matter whether you call that higher power by the name of God, Allah, Jesus, Brahman, Krishna, Buddha, the Tao, Ahura Mazda, Elohim, Ein Sof, the Great Spirit, or any other name, or whether you see that higher power as the consciousness and awareness of the Universe, which I refer to as All-That-Is. The Universe doesn't care how you refer to it.

The crystallization of the concepts I perceived that day in Hawaii was due, in part, to an intense desire I have to live in a world where everything is perfect. I want to believe that we live in a Universe where everything that occurs and does not occur is for our complete benefit. I want to believe in a perfectly balanced, perfectly ordered Universe. I want to believe in a Universe where, even though I am a tiny part of it, I am important and you are important—a Universe where, more than just important, we are special beings, able to direct our own courses, able to evolve spiritually to higher planes of existence. I want to believe that our spirit has a personality and that the personality survives when it is our time for transformation to the next phase through the doorway we call death. I want to believe that, as a part of the eternal Universe, we too are eternal. I want to believe these things and, as a result of my wanting, I continually search for evidence that supports the way I want things to be.

I have found that evidence, and therefore I believe that the events that come into our lives are perfect and are for our total benefit. Because we are the Universe, a part of it, and because the Universe is fully aware, fully present, fully conscious of you and me, it will only permit events to occur in our lives that are totally beneficial. And because the Universe continues in a moment-by-moment unfolding of new events, it is always necessary to acknowledge the rightness, the perfection of those new events in order to keep in step with the ever-unfolding, ever-changing Universe. So I keep nodding my head in agreement as I move along through life, witnessing the ever-unfolding Universe.

LEAVE LAMENTING BEHIND

When you look at all events as having a purpose and know that that purpose is to benefit you, when you agree with their absolute perfection, you are harmonizing yourself with your Universe and you will then be in a better state of mind to handle events more capably because you will already be in step with what "is."

Imagine a string of events coming into your life over the period of a day, each one demanding that you make an appropriate decision for your continued success. The first event causes an all-consuming anger within you. The next event comes ten minutes later and it demands a rational, coolheaded decision, but you are still consumed by anger over the first event. The third event comes right behind the second, again demanding a rational decision, and you ignore it because you are still involved with your anger. The same is true with the fourth, fifth, and sixth events that you continue to ignore, leading to the downfall of your potential success. Later on, you discover that the first event that consumed you with anger was actually for your benefit. And then you say what everyone says: "If I had only known . . . " That brings to mind a bit of a poem by John Greenleaf Whittier: "For of all sad words of tongue or pen, the saddest are these: 'It might have been!'"

Your involvement with the first event can be likened to many events that have occurred in your life. You, like everyone, have spent many hours, days, weeks, and even years lamenting past events that were actually for your complete benefit from the first moment. All that lamenting—for nothing. All those precious minutes when life slipped by in all its glory, its wonder—lost, while you were stuck in your hurtful and possibly hateful emotions. If tragedies could exist, that loss would head the list. This book is freeing you from all that, so carefully fulfill the exercises; they are the means to your liberation.

In 2007, I was in New York giving interviews for my book *The Alcoholism and Addiction Cure*. When one of the reporters who interviewed me came to the interview, I could smell alcohol on his breath. I mentioned it and he said, yes, he drank every day. I asked him why he did that and he said it was because he was the victim of a missed opportunity early on in his life. I asked him to tell me about it.

The reporter said that when he was twenty-five he had an opportunity to go to the world-famous Harvard University in Cambridge, Massachusetts, but he chose not to go. He said that now he was only a part-time reporter and that his regular job was driving a food-delivery truck six days a week starting at three in the morning. He said he hated it. He blamed his early decision not to attend Harvard for his current unhappy job situation. I asked him if he was married and he told me that he was married and had six children. I asked if he loved his wife and children. He said they were the joy of his life, the best thing that had ever happened to him.

I asked him if he had gone to another college, and he said he had but it was a small, virtually unknown college. I asked if anything unusual had happened at that college and he said, "Yes, that's where I met my wife." I was amazed. "And you're unhappy that you didn't go to Harvard?" I exclaimed. "You must be a madman! That's the best thing that ever happened to you!" I saw that all his years of disappointment had been over an event that was, in reality, a huge benefit to him. After he thought about it a minute, he said, "You know, you're quite right." A few months later, I received a letter from his sister telling me that her brother had quit drinking and was a changed man.

THE MOMENT OF CHOICE

Events are just events. How you perceive those events and respond to them determines their outcome in your life. What dictates how you respond to events is your personal philosophy. You are in charge of that.

A philosophy is defined as a system of beliefs, attitudes, or concepts that guides an individual, or as the study of the principles and laws that regulate the Universe and underlie all knowledge and all reality. Take a moment to think about that: the study of principles and laws *that regulate the Universe and underlie all knowledge and all reality*.

Your personal philosophy is what you believe to be true about the world in which you live. As you read earlier, it is essential that you live according to a guiding personal philosophy, a lodestar, that will see you through the difficult times of despair, hardship, grief, and despondency that regularly occur in your life. A philosophy that will give you strength, composure, patience, and durability. A philosophy that will highlight your good times and turn them into exceptional times. A philosophy that will change your down feelings into cheerful feelings and bring a smile to your face. And that smile will be more than a brave veneer in the face of adversity; it will be the smile of one who knows that the mystery of the adversity will soon unravel itself, revealing a happy and perfect ending that will show that the adversity was for your total benefit.

A weak philosophy is a weak way of life. A strong philosophy, based on what is true in the Universe, withstands all the rigors and tests of time. This is your time to create a powerful, joy-giving, happiness-sustaining philosophy.

Consider for a moment my experience with the fishhook and what could have happened as an alternative to what did happen. Suppose the instant the fishhook plunged into my finger I had become enraged, grabbed the string, and tore the hook from my finger, ripping the flesh. Suppose that my thoughtless, angry act had enraged me still further and I had cursed my luck and kicked the rocks. It's possible that because of my rage, I could have fallen and lost my life at that spot. That's far-fetched, but it is a possibility.

Now consider what did happen. The instant the fishhook pierced my finger, I acknowledged the event with "Perfect!" After all, the event was over. It was impossible to back up time and rearrange my actions so that the event would never have taken place. What could I do? Only one thing—react to it. That's the *only* option open to each of us after *every* event. How I reacted was up to me. I could have either reacted in a way that would have brought out the potential good of the situation and maintained my superb feeling of the day, or I could have cursed my luck and brought out the negative side of the experience. It was my moment of choice, the same moment that is there for all of us when an event occurs.

Suppose you suffered a painful experience that caused you to discover a truth that blessed your life from that time forward. Would you curse the "accident" or call it "good fortune"? Each incident in life basically provides just those two choices. Only with that knowledge as a major part of your philosophy will you be able to proceed through life swiftly, surely, and successfully. Only with that philosophy will you achieve deep, lasting happiness. That belief alone will enable you to see the happy side of seemingly unhappy events and give you the insight to see future events in an optimistic, knowledgeable way.

Consider what the word *perfect* means. The dictionary defines it as whole, complete, or without flaw. To that I would add my own definition: "That which cannot be improved by adding to it or taking away from it." The concept that things are "perfect" is not difficult to understand, but putting into use the concept that "everything that happens to me is perfect and is for my total benefit" can be difficult. It requires more than just an intellectual understanding.

First, it requires you to accept all that happens as perfect: wars, the splinter in your finger, earthquakes, disasters of every kind, death, injury, loss of loved ones, loss of love, lost opportunity, physical traumas, rape, deception, guilt for things you did to others for which you cannot forgive yourself, abandonment, betrayal, theft, and loss of possessions, just to name a few. Next, it requires you to have the patience that goes with your belief in perfection. Even in the face of what you would normally think of as rotten luck, you must be patient, reacting as though it were the best luck possible, knowing that you will soon find out why it was the best luck possible.

If you ever want to be truly happy, you must give up feelings of resentment and rage because you cannot feel happy while those feelings are present. You get to choose. You can't have them both at the same time. Which one do you want?

"THAT'S PERFECT"

Your reward for following the empowering philosophy that everything that happens is for your benefit is an increasing, conscious control over all situations and a far more pleasurable now, heightened by your vision of a bright and happy future. You will also be rewarded with memories of a pleasurable past as you see yourself following your philosophy with sureness. By keeping in mind the consequences of your responses, you'll create happiness-producing results.

Suppose you are feeling really good and are having a fine day when someone drives his car over your bicycle. If you say, "That's perfect!" and mean it, you will be responding to the incident as though it were a good thing for you. What happens? It's a law of the Universe that every action produces a result. Because the Universe is forced to respond to you as you are being at every moment, when you respond positively you bring out the event's more pleasant aspects, its positive potential, which you then experience. On the other hand, if you react to the broken bicycle, or any event, as though you are the victim of bad luck, you are, in effect, forcing the Universe to respond to you as if you really were a victim. You will perceive the Universe's reaction as more bad luck, but, in actuality, you are causing that response by your initial reaction.

To understand how this works, let's play out the broken-bike scenario in a very exaggerated way. First, imagine that when you see the car running over your bike, you run out of your house, drag the driver out of the car, and have a fight. The police come and you're taken to jail, where you are sexually molested. You kill the person who molested you and you are sentenced to life imprisonment. That's one option.

Here's another. You walk over to the driver's side of the car. The driver is waiting apprehensively for your reaction. You smile and say, "That was just right—don't worry." Your unexpected reaction produces a rush of gratitude from the driver. You introduce yourself and the grateful driver offers to pay for the damaged bike. Your response is "That's fine. I'll accept the payment, but let's take a moment and see if this event occurred because we needed to meet." You and the driver get to know each other and become lifelong friends.

You marry his sister, have a wonderful family, and spend many years together in great pleasure. Additionally, suppose that, unbeknownst to you, the bolt that held the front tire on your bike was loose and the next time you rode it you would have had a serious accident going down a steep hill.

Give the Universe credit for knowing exactly what you need in order to have the greatest life possible. Trust the Universe. Give every event the chance to prove its absolute necessity for being in your life so it can bring you major benefits. The way to do that is to greet every event as a gift from your loving, caring, totally knowledgeable Universe.

Act according to the philosophy that every event unfolds only to benefit you completely and you'll cause every event to continue itself along those lines. The following story perfectly illustrates how your new philosophy will work to sustain, enlighten, and protect you every day of your life. It is taken from my book *The Alcoholism and Addiction Cure*.

Each of us has suffered in our lifetime. We've been lied to, we've been betrayed and cheated, and we've been taken advantage of. Many of us, perhaps you, have been beaten, raped, mistreated, forced to do things against our will, or sexually molested by parents, siblings, or strangers. We've had our hearts broken and we've suffered great financial, spiritual, and physical losses. We've grieved over the loss of loved ones and we've been born with physical or mental deformities. How we deal with those traumas and others like them will determine our state of happiness today or, for that matter, any day.

A few years ago, Peter, a twenty-five-year-old athlete, checked into Passages Addiction Cure Center in Malibu, California, the treatment center that my son Pax and I cofounded and codirect. He was psychologically addicted to using marijuana. Peter was particularly interested in my weekly metaphysics sessions. He loved the philosophy portion of those groups and took it to heart. He and I also had several one-on-one sessions. In those sessions, he learned what you're learning here. At the end of his thirty-day stay, his marijuana dependency was cured. A few months after he left Passages, Peter had an accident and is now paralyzed from the waist down and confined to a wheelchair. Two days after his accident, I went to see him in the hospital. When I walked into the room, his eyes lit up and he said in a quiet voice, "Don't worry, I know this is the best thing that could have happened to me."

Today, he persists in that belief. We talk every few months and he tells me of the heights to which his enlightenment has soared. He says that his spiritual growth could never have come so far in such a short time without his accident. He's an inspiration to all who meet him and he occasionally visits us and speaks at meetings of Passages alumni.

How did you feel about Peter's response when I walked into his hospital room and he said, "This is the best thing that could have happened to me"? Did you say to yourself, sarcastically, "Yeah, right!" as if nothing could possibly be further from the truth? To the degree that you reacted that way, your personal philosophy is different from the one that's sustaining Peter and his peaceful feeling while he sits in his wheelchair. It means that you probably regard all incidents that seem unlucky as *actually* unlucky. But it's mainly because of that thinking that your current circumstances have come about.

To add a bit more to the story that has unfolded in the years since I wrote about this enlightened young man, Peter has now married the nurse who cares for him and he has recently invited me to play tennis with him. He is a "special athlete" and plays from his wheelchair. His joy remains unabated.

Think of the difference between Peter's vision of what happened to him as opposed to someone else in a similar situation who reacted by becoming an alcoholic or drug addict, continually lamenting his "bad luck." That person sits in his wheelchair, drunk, unshaven, dressed sloppily, and in messy surroundings, while Peter is out with his wife, playing tennis in his wheelchair.

In the face of *every* new situation you encounter, you get to choose one of those two lifestyles. By reading this and creating a personal philosophy for yourself that is in line with "Everything that happens is the best possible thing that can happen to me," you will be safe from falling into the trap of feeling like a victim.

SWITCHING TRACKS

In the beginning, questions will arise in your mind that might weaken your newly awakening belief that every event is for your benefit. What about the innocent child born with birth defects? What about disease and sickness? What about the bombs dropped on all those innocent people in all those wars?

Questions like those are ones you will be able to answer for yourself after you have lived with your philosophy, when it has seen you through times of despair and pain, softened the hard times, and highlighted and brightened even your best days. In this time of *new beginning*, of *new awakening*, content yourself with seeing perfection in the lost watch, the disappointing friendship, the dented fender, the stubbed toe (an acupuncture point needed release), and the missed bus or plane. Start with what is easiest, and one day you will also see what is hardest as "perfect."

Adopting as part of your philosophy the belief that *"I am a perfect being in a perfect Universe, where everything that happens benefits me completely"* will benefit you greatly. *You* are the doorway through which your life unfolds. *You* are the mechanism by which your life is controlled. Remember, when you react to events in a way that causes you more unpleasantness, the unpleasantness you experience will appear to confirm that what happened was truly unfortunate. Yet, in reality, it was your *reaction* to the event that caused the continuation of the unpleasantness.

You can think of it in this way: You're like a railroad switch. Each time an event occurs, you channel the continuing stream of events onto the positive or negative track. Even though the event hurt you, shamed you, or took something away from you, you are still in charge of switching it onto a positive or negative track. You determine its future outcome.

Sometime in your life something happened to you that seemed awful, but days, weeks, or even years later, you said, "That was the best thing that could have happened to me." That is true for everyone. Condition yourself to see that truth the moment each event occurs. Learn to see that perfect truth now. Know that "rotten luck" is a falsehood. It's like the man who drove the food-delivery truck; his choice not to go to Harvard University led to his attending that small, little-known college where he met his future wife, the love of his life, with whom he now has six wonderful children.

It may be hard to believe that the banged toe, the torn clothing, the lost watch, or the stolen wallet is completely beneficial for you, but that is why there are so few people who are happy and who have their life the way they want it. Act positively and the events coming after will be positive, and you will then get to enjoy those positive events. As you progress along this path, you will feel a rising tide of enthusiasm and expectation welling up within you. Let it come!

EXERCISE NUMBER ONE

Building a New Philosophy

In the space below, under the heading "My Philosophy," write:

I am a perfect being in a perfect Universe, where everything that happens benefits me completely.

Sign your name and write the date at the bottom of the page.

My Philosophy:

Signature:________________________________ **Date:**__________

EXERCISE NUMBER TWO

Seeing All Events as Beneficial

Spend the rest of today and all of tomorrow viewing the events that you experience as perfect. Call them perfect and treat them that way. Actively look for events and be deliberate in labeling them as just right for you—perfect events brought into your life by an aware Universe so that you can receive a benefit. The hardest part is *keeping aware*, remembering what your job is for today and tomorrow. It is so easy to become caught up in a situation or an event and forget to see it through the eyes of awareness.

The Boy Scouts have an inner organization called the Order of the Arrow. During a three-day initiation, the chosen candidates must remain silent. They wear a small wooden arrow on a string around their necks. Each time one is caught speaking, a notch is cut into the arrow. At the third speaking offense, the arrow is broken and the candidate is refused admittance to the order. To help themselves remember to keep silent, most of the candidates hold the arrow between their teeth—especially after they have been caught talking the second time!

Find some memory aid to assist you in keeping aware that you are to see everything that happens today and tomorrow as being totally beneficial to you. At Passages Addiction Cure Center, we provide our clients with a blue rubber bracelet with the words *It's Perfect* printed on it in white. Passages is the world's most successful center for curing dependency on alcohol, prescription medication, street drugs, and other forms of addictive behavior, such as sex and gambling addictions. We attribute a great deal of the success of our clients to the life-transforming philosophy they learn at Passages, the same one you are learning here.

To help you remember your task in this exercise, perhaps you can carry a small stone or this book in your hand. Avoid tying a string on your finger as a memory aid; most people quickly forget it's there. If you elect to help yourself remember by carrying a small stone, this book, or some other object, then carry it all the time. When that object becomes inconvenient or difficult to carry is exactly when you will most need it to serve as your memory aid.

Once your mind becomes focused on whatever you are doing to help yourself remember, then replace the focus of your attention with the idea that *all events are perfect and benefit me completely*.

Whatever it takes for you to stay aware for today and tomorrow is what you should do. Seeing things in a good light, a perfect light, is the heart of the personal philosophy you are creating for yourself.

EXERCISE NUMBER THREE

Three Minutes of Perfection

This is a practice session to assist you in training your mind to react to events and circumstances in a way that will bring you the greatest possible benefit. It will free you from the negative side of life, opening you to the tremendous benefits that are available in every situation. It is essential that you train your mind to immediately look for the benefits in every situation in which you find yourself. After a while, it gets to be a habit, and when everyone around you is in turmoil, you're calm and happy, looking for the part of the situation that is going to be of great benefit to you, *knowing it's there*. In those moments, you will love yourself for having found your new philosophy.

Find a comfortable place and sit quietly for just three minutes. Close your eyes and imagine yourself seeing that everything you read, hear about, or experience in any way is perfect for you. See yourself switching the "negative" things you see and hear to a positive track. Imagine seemingly bad events, and see yourself knowing they are for your total and complete benefit, understanding that the only reason the events occurred is so that you can benefit.

Do this every day for twenty-five days. Mark your calendar now. Check off a day on your calendar each time you complete a three-minute exercise. You may continue this beyond twenty-five days if you wish, and you may spend more time than three minutes.

This part of the program will train your mind to look for and to find the positive side of events and give you an outlook on life that will delight you day in and day out. It will also allow you to grasp the opportunity in situations long before anyone else does.

EXERCISE NUMBER FOUR

Changing Your Reaction to the Past

Find a comfortable place and sit quietly for fifteen minutes. Let your mind wander back through your past, remembering three seemingly unfortunate events that you have experienced. Spend some time thinking about what happened. Then see those events as though they were completely beneficial to you. Even if you don't yet know how you have benefited or will benefit, imagine each event to be that way. Perhaps you learned a valuable lesson or the event led to another circumstance that turned out to be extremely positive.

In the beginning, you may have to pretend, but your job is to keep seeing them as "perfect," as "just right" for you. It may be difficult if you have, for instance, been in a severe auto accident and lost a leg, an arm, your sight, or someone close to you, but you must persevere in this exercise until you get it right—really right. No halfway measures will work. This is the only way you will ever free yourself from the negative thoughts that are currently in your mind with regard to past events. *Never give in to seeing yourself as a victim*. Giving in or giving up are the real disasters. The more you have difficulty with this exercise, the more you need it.

After you have done the first part of this exercise, think of later events that gave you pleasure and realize that the seemingly bad events were part of a chain of circumstances that led you to the pleasurable events or circumstances. The pleasurable events were a direct result of the seemingly bad events.

For instance, you may have had your heart broken earlier in life, but later you may have found a new partner and experienced a wonderful love relationship. Know that the second relationship would not have happened without the first relationship ending. Know that the heartbreak was part of the experience you needed to have in order to be able to comprehend what you are learning here today.

The Universe is that intricate, that well thought-out, and that far-seeing. Those seemingly negative events were leading you to this moment in time, where you are learning to be who you want and have what you want. Without those events, you may have never read this book. Life is like that. One event leads to another in an unbroken chain, and the chain is "your life." Live it to the fullest. Know you're in the best hands of all—those of the Universe—and that you are an integral, inseparable part of that Universe.

This exercise is an important part of the chain of events in your life. You must come to totally believe that the later, good events that came into your life were part of and were a direct result of the same chain of events as those seemingly unfortunate events. If you give up before you have accomplished this exercise, you'll be giving in to feelings of despair and despondency and all you'll get is despair and despondency. Treat yourself to some good feelings. If fifteen minutes is not enough time for you to accomplish this, take longer or use several fifteen-minute sessions.

The past will still be the past and the events will remain the same, but you will feel differently about them and you will react differently when you think of them. The same holds true for events and circumstances that are now in your life. Look at events that are causing you emotional hurt or anger in a new way, a way that will cause you to have good feelings about them. It's tough, but you can do it. Pretend if you have to, but do it.

To feel frustration, anger, or other hurtful emotions is to carry burdens. Who would willfully carry burdens, particularly when they are not burdens at all but just events and situations masquerading as burdens? It may be hard for you to change how you see current events in your life if you are lying in bed recovering from a near-fatal auto accident, but you must do it. You have chosen in the past to feel the hurt, the emotional pain, or the anger, but now *let it go!* Replace those feelings with good feelings about what happened. Free yourself.

Do this exercise today and then on the following Wednesdays and Saturdays for four weeks. Mark your calendar now. You may move ahead to the next chapter after you have accomplished one of these fifteen-minute sessions.

EXERCISE NUMBER FIVE

Learning to Be Happy—Pleasure Exercise #4

Enjoy another half hour of pleasure. Begin by saying, *"I, [say your name], give myself permission to enjoy a half hour of pleasure."* Fulfill this exercise indoors.

Remember, if it turns out to be less than pleasurable, start over or choose another pleasure exercise. When you've completed this exercise, write a brief summary on the next page under the heading "Pleasure Exercise #4" along with the date you completed the exercise.

Complete the exercises in this chapter before going on to chapter 6.

Pleasure Exercise #4:

Date completed: ______________________________

6

YOU ARE THE CENTER

You have your brush, you have your colors,
you paint paradise, then—in you go.
—Nikos Kazantzakis

ONE OF THE LAWS OF OUR UNIVERSE IS CHANGE. That law provides that *everything* in the Universe will be in a *constant* state of change—everything except the laws of the Universe. To some extent, you participate in that ever-unfolding change. Say that you live on a farm where there is a stream, and you widen it and deepen it so that it becomes a pond. You put some fish, some frogs, and some lily pads in the pond, and you plant a tree on its edge whose branches hang over and trail in the water. As a result of your actions, birds build their nests in the tree, wild ducks land on the pond, and wild animals come to drink. The grass grows, the fish and frogs multiply, and nature fulfills itself. As you can see, by building the pond, you have participated in the continuing creation of the world around you.

Say that you are a teacher and the children whose lives you influence take up occupations such as doctors, farmers, biologists, scientists, presidents, engineers, carpenters, and other callings of their choosing. From that point forward, both the children and the Universe will be forever different because you existed. If you throw a pebble into the ocean, you will cause the level of the ocean to rise—not much, but rise it will.

You may not think of yourself as the center of the Universe, and you're most likely not, but you can see from these simple examples how you play a role in shaping the world around you. Yet there is a Universe where you play more than a minor role. In that Universe, you are the center and you are the key player. I call it your "personal Universe." It is that portion of the Universe that affects you personally. If the sun shines and you get a sunburn, you have been affected by your Universe. If you assist someone, and years later they do you a favor, you have affected your personal Universe and have been affected by your personal Universe. Your personal Universe exists *only* because you exist. If you didn't exist, neither would your personal Universe. In other words, if you were absent from your personal Universe, your personal Universe would be absent as well. In *that* Universe, you *are* the center.

Being the center is more than being *at* the center. If you were only *at* the center, when you moved, you would move away from the center. *Being* the center means that as you move, the center moves with you. It is only when you are fully aware that you are the center of your personal Universe—creating and influencing *everything* around you by being how you're being at every moment—that you will understand the importance of your every thought and act.

Take a moment now to imagine yourself as the center of your personal Universe. Imagine that everything you say, do, and think affects everyone and everything around you.

Holding that image in your mind will cause you to take care with your every action, with your every thought, and with everything you say because you will know that you are producing far-reaching effects that will bring you results that are exactly in accord with what you put out there.

THE MAGIC WORDS

I am going to tell you a story that will help you understand what can happen when you fully accept the idea that you have a personal Universe and that you are in control of what happens there. You'll also understand a bit more about what is meant by the ancient saying "a journey of a thousand miles begins with a single step."

In the spring of 1970, I was sitting with my eleven-year-old son, Todd, at a funky outdoor restaurant at the top of Topanga Canyon in Southern California. We had our dog with us, a 105-pound black Lab/Shepherd named Crash. Crash was unique to us in that he had carried his retrieval instincts to great heights and was never happy unless someone was participating with him in his favorite game of looking for hidden objects. We loved Crash and wanted to share him with the rest of the world. So, sitting there on that fine spring day, I suggested to Todd that we write a story about Crash. He agreed.

"Okay," I said, "this is a story about a boy and his dog, and you're a boy, so how about you tell me what this story is about." Todd said that he didn't know how to tell a story. Then I asked him the question that initiated what was to become one of the most exciting adventures of our lives.

"Where would you like the story to begin?" I said.

"In the swamp!" he promptly replied.

"The swamp?" I asked incredulously. "You've never been in a swamp."

"That's okay. I want to start in the swamp."

I told him about the great swamp in the Everglades of Florida, and he thought that was a fine place to begin. I then asked him the second fateful question.

"Where else would you like the story to take place?"

"I like the Pacific Northwest," he said.

I asked how he proposed to take his story from the Everglades in Florida to the Pacific Northwest. And he replied with his fateful answer: *"We could run away."*

During the next two hours, Todd outlined an incredible story that would start us on a journey that would completely occupy my life for the next seven years.

One of our good friends was a man of about fifty whom we called "Big Frank." Big Frank was a good-natured giant who stood six feet eight inches tall in his stocking feet and weighed in at just over three hundred pounds. He was hugely powerful and he was also simpleminded. We loved him and he loved us. We were almost his only close friends. Of course, Todd elected to have Big Frank accompany the boy on his imaginary journey across the country.

We worked on the story all spring and most of the summer. To be undisturbed, we took a train to Mexico City, where we stayed for three weeks and worked every day on the story. We returned with the story nearly finished. We were sitting on the beach in Malibu, putting the finishing touches to the story, when Todd said, "This would make a great Disney film."

"You're right," I replied. "Let's go talk to them." We left

the beach in jeans, tee shirts, and sneakers and drove to Disney Studios in Burbank. There was a guard at the parking lot gate, so we parked outside, waited until he was out of sight, and then scooted in to the reception office.

The woman behind the desk asked how she could help us. The conversation went like this:

"We want to see someone about making a movie," I told her.

"Do you have an appointment with someone?"

"No."

"How did you get in here past the guard?"

"We're supposed to be here," I said. I knew that because we *were* there.

"Well, I don't know how to help you."

"Well, I suppose we want to rent a camera crew. Who's the head of the camera department?"

When the receptionist told us the name of the man in charge, I said, "Good. Please call him and tell him we'd like to talk to him." She called around to several departments looking for him, and one of the departments was the production department.

"Wait!" I said when I heard that. "Forget about the camera department. I want to talk to the man who is the head of the production department."

"Mr. John Bloss is the head of that department, but you can't see him," she responded.

"Why not?"

"Because he's a very important man and he has appointments scheduled three weeks ahead."

"That's okay. You call him and tell him we're out here and he'll see us."

"Who are you?"

"I'm Chris Prentiss, and this is my son, Todd."

Then she asked the million-dollar question: "And who are you with?"

I thought to myself, "I'm with Todd," but I replied in a flash of inspiration, "Prentiss Productions."

In an awed tone, the receptionist said, "You're the head of it?"

I thought to myself, between Todd and me, I'm the head of it, so I told her, "That's correct, I'm the head of it."

The receptionist picked up the phone, got John Bloss on the line, and, again in an awed tone, as if I were the head of Paramount Studios, said, "Mr. Bloss, Mr. Prentiss is here to see you, and he's the *head* of Prentiss Productions." After a short pause, she said, "Mr. Bloss is asking what you want."

"Tell him I want him to tell me how to make a movie."

Ten minutes later, when Todd and I were shown into his office, he was prostrate on his couch with laughter thinking about the head of Prentiss Productions who had come asking how to make a film.

In that meeting, John Bloss and I became good friends. Todd and I spent two hours telling him about the story of a boy, his dog, and his great friend who made their way across the country, a jump ahead of the police, looking for home—not the home they ran away from, but a new home where they could find peace. We called the story *Goin' Home*.

I asked John if he thought it would make a good Disney film and he said he was sure of it. I told him that Big Frank was a real person and Crash was a real dog. He asked how many dogs we had and I said, "One." I thought that was a ridiculous question until he told me we should have at least six dogs that looked alike. He told me there were nine Lassies. He asked what would happen if they were halfway through the film, had spent forty million dollars, and the dog was hit by a car. The studio couldn't take that kind of risk, he explained. Then I asked if we could use Big Frank and Todd, but he said no, they wanted professional actors. I asked if I could direct the film and he said no, they needed a professional director.

I thought about that for a few moments and then said it didn't sound like much fun for Todd and me. He agreed and then said the magic words: "Why don't you make the film yourself?"

When I asked how I would start to do that, he told me I would need a top-notch production manager, who would make up for what I didn't know. He gave me the name of someone who was making a film on location for Disney in Canada, along with the man's phone number at his hotel. I stood up and shook hands with John and bid him goodbye. He asked, "Where are you going?" to which I replied, "Canada."

IN THE FACE OF EVERY IMAGINABLE ADVERSITY

It was time for Todd to go back to school, so I put him on a plane and sent him off to New Jersey, where he lived with his mom. Then I drove to Canada and met the production manager. He loved the film story and had some great ideas, but he didn't like some of the ideas I had that were quite new to filmmaking. So when I left, I decided not to work with him.

I didn't know what would happen to a boy and his dog on the road making their way across America, so I put Crash on a plane with me and we flew to Miami, Florida. A friend picked me up there and drove me to the beginning of the highway called the Tamiami Trail, which crosses lower Florida at the Everglades.

I had a sixty-pound pack on my back and I started off. I walked about a hundred feet before I was huffing and puffing, and I felt as if I was being cut in two by the straps of the pack. I put the pack down, adjusted the straps, and started off again. This time I only got about fifty feet. Several more attempts only gained me about a hundred yards.

There was a car parked on a side street and its driver had been watching my progress. He pulled out, drove past me, peering at me, then turned around and stopped and asked where I was going. When I told him Seattle, Washington, he laughed so hard that tears came to his eyes. He told me to get in and he would drive me about twenty miles to the beginning of the seventy-five-mile toll road that led to the west side of Florida. I began to tell him the script story of the boy and his dog and Big Frank, and he got so involved in hearing it that he drove me all the way across Florida.

That was the start of the fortuitous events that would be the heart of the trip Crash and I would take across America. We spent forty-nine days on the road, hitching rides, hiking, kayaking down the Colorado River, sleeping outdoors every night in a tent, and finding out what might happen to a boy and his dog on the run across the country. We had great adventures, but those are for another story.

It was evident to me that there was something watching out for us. My understanding of the Universe and how it works, its awareness and consciousness, was in an earlier stage, so I was not fully aware of its operation in my life. But I knew something of it and was grateful for the little I knew. Even though we were out there alone traveling across the country, I felt safe. So I do know how it can feel just learning about all of this. In a way, this book is a rocket-to-the-moon course in what the Universe is really like and will save you the decades it took me to become fully aware of that.

I cannot tell you why I was so completely committed to making this film, but I felt a total commitment to my project that was stronger than anything I had ever felt in the previous thirty-four years of my life. At some point during the writing of the story with Todd, I decided that I would finish making the film in the face of every imaginable adversity and even the ones I couldn't imagine. I was totally committed. As it turned out, I would need every ounce of that commitment before I finished the film, six years later.

After Crash and I arrived in Seattle, I hailed a cab, drove to the airport and took a plane to Los Angeles. After that trip, I needed to be alone to write the script, so I got an Indian teepee and put it up on an isolated mountaintop in Southern California, where I lived for nine months while I wrote the script.

It was in February of 1972 that I finally began filming. Having never made a film before, having no experience whatsoever apart from having gone to the movies, and being undercapitalized from the outset, I ran into enormous difficulties. The day before the thirty-five man crew and I were to leave for Florida, money I had expected to be invested in my project didn't materialize, but I had already bought plane tickets for everyone to get to Florida, where I had sent the equipment, the cameras, the trucks, and a bus for transportation. I called the crew together and told them we had no money. The director of photography asked me if we had enough money for six or seven weeks. I told him that we had enough money for six or seven days. When he asked me what I was going to do, I told him and the crew that I had already sent all the equipment to Florida and I was going to go there and make a film. I told them I didn't know how I was going to do it, but that I was going. And if they weren't going, I would find a new crew in Florida. They had a private meeting and came in and said that they knew it was crazy, but they were all going with me.

That trip would be the first of three attempts I made to film across the country. I made it from Naples, Florida, to New Orleans, Louisiana. Every night when we were finished filming, I would get on the phone and call potential investors to raise enough money to keep us going. In New Orleans, I ran out of money and had to send the crew home along with the cast members. They were incredibly disappointed because they knew we were making a good film.

It never entered my mind, though, to think of myself as beaten or to quit my project. Instead, I had the film editor edit the one-third of the movie I had filmed, and I took it to England, where I negotiated a distribution agreement that gave me some breathing room. It took two more years, but in 1974 I pulled together enough money and resources to start again.

During the first trip, I had put together a fully professional union crew, which *Boxoffice* magazine reported as being one of the best crews to leave Hollywood to work on a film in ten years. The crew I hired for this second phase of the production was not nearly as experienced but a lot less expensive. We began again at the southern tip of Florida, but I had a major setback when I arrived there with the cast and crew. *Big Frank wouldn't come to work*. He had some silly reason, which I don't even remember, but I could not talk him into coming to Florida. He said he was finished with filmmaking. I understood why. He was extremely shy, and getting in front of a camera was a terror to him.

So there I was with a thirty-five man crew, the cast, and no Big Frank. Not only that, but the inexperienced crew was used to working with a tightly written script that they would study in preparation for filming the next day. With no Big Frank, we had no script and they panicked. The night before we were to start filming, they told me it was impossible for them to film without a script and they wanted to go home.

You can imagine my desperation, with just a small amount of money, film and supplies to buy, so many people to house, feed, and transport, and now this. Well, I have persuasive powers that I am told are unusually great. I convinced them that I could create a script as we went along and that I would find actors and situations that would be even better than the script I had written when Big Frank was in the film, if only they would trust me.

Although they agreed to stay with me, they grumbled and complained the whole time. This trip across the country found me on the verge of despair almost continually as I fought the crew, the weather, the lack of money, and all the thousand and one difficulties that are part of making any film. However, in thirteen weeks of filming, we made it to Big Sur, the ending place of the film, and the crew went home. I have never been so glad to say goodbye to anyone.

I went back to Los Angeles and rented an editing studio at the end of a pier in Malibu, hired a former Disney editor, and worked with him for six months while we put together the film. After all of that work, however, I was not happy with the finished product and decided to reshoot the entire film. You might think I was crazy and that I would have decided to cut my losses then and there. But I knew that I was supposed to make this film and that Todd was supposed to be a part of it. Just because things had not gone the way I expected didn't mean I was powerless.

In planning my third attempt, the thought of again having to fight with a cameraman to get the shots I would need was so abhorrent to me that I decided to make a major gamble and film it myself. I put together a tiny crew of six people, hired all the equipment and a big semi truck to carry it in, and I began filming again with Todd at the southern tip of Florida. This time, though, I had the script that I had already written for the version of the film I had just finished editing.

I was filled with trepidation when we set up the big Mitchell 35mm camera and I prepared to make my first shot. But when I looked through the camera, I was totally amazed; I saw exactly what I would expect to see on the screen when the film was finished. I realized that what you see is what you get! The director of photography I had hired for the first trip, who had worked on some of the greatest films ever made, later viewed the film I shot during that time and said that the photography was as good as anything he had ever seen. You see, I was supposed to make this film and I was supposed to shoot it, and the Universe gave me the inspiration and resources to do both.

IN THE ARENA

Filming is an unusual business, to say the least. It is a project that will literally suck you dry, taking all your talent, all your money, all your assets, and all your strength, and scream for more. A small moment in time from that journey will give you an idea what it was like. More importantly, it will show you what can happen when you take charge of your personal Universe. And it will show you the huge potential that exists when you are aware that every event, no matter how dire it seems, holds an opportunity and a gift for you. It is *you* who determine the outcomes in your life, not another.

We were in New Orleans, the same city where I was forced to abandon my first attempt to cross the country. The situation was difficult because I had spent almost all of the available money. Funds I had expected to be invested in the film had failed to materialize, and I owed more than $15,000 to the hotel where the cast and crew were staying. I had used up every credit source and asset available to me. Despair was again riding heavily on my shoulders. I had come so far, and now it seemed as if I would suffer the same defeat in the same town where I had been forced to send the crew home the first time.

I was again fighting for money, time, film, equipment, lodging, and transportation, while at the same time directing and photographing a sensitive film about a boy and his dog looking for home. With every source of cash and credit used up and two thousand more miles to go, I couldn't see how it was possible to complete the project.

When the cast and crew finished a day's work and went in for dinner, I would head for my room and the telephone to make arrangements for the next day's transportation, the next meal, the next bit of film, the next lodging, the next source of money. Filming is an up-before-dawn business and, beyond having to deal with the money problem, I was exhausted. Many nights, utter exhaustion would overtake me, and I would fall asleep in the midst of a telephone conversation.

As you might imagine, I was having a hard time believing that those circumstances were for my benefit. My developing philosophy was in its early stages and I was feeling extremely depressed. But I knew that it was my job to keep on with it—it was my now. The script I had written called for filming on the Mississippi River, and I had two tug boats standing by, one to be filmed and one to use as a platform for filming. The tugs cost thousands of dollars a day to rent, and I had only enough money for one day. At the end of twenty-four hours of straight filming, we weren't finished. I went to the owner of the tugs and told him what the situation required. I told him that I needed more time, and since I was out of cash, other arrangements were necessary. I offered him a share in the film profits, telling him that he might get more of what he wanted, which was money, by giving me more of what I wanted, which was the use of the tug boats.

We avoided becoming opponents. Instead, we became two people who wanted the same thing—to get the movie made. He agreed to let me use the boats, but only for one more filming session. We could keep the tugs as long as we were filming. We took the tugboats up the Mississippi, filming day scenes and night scenes as the sun rose and set. We filmed continuously for forty hours. For most people, that's an entire week of work. When at last my eyes actually became too tired to focus when looking through the camera lens, I had to order the tugs home, even though we weren't finished.

My fatigued condition must have impressed the tugboat owner because he let us use the tugs for another day. We slept seven hours, filmed for a continuous twenty-six hours, and still we needed more time! Again, he granted us another day. We slept six hours and filmed another twenty-six hours and finally completed the river scenes.

On the way back down the Mississippi, I was wobbling from exhaustion when a crew member came to me and reported that one of the cast we had recruited from New Orleans as an extra for the hobo scene had fallen overboard and was likely drowned. It was a blow that I felt would be almost impossible to recover from. I fell into bed and had slept only seven hours when I was awakened by my production manager, who was holding up the front page of *The Times-Picayune*, New Orleans' major newspaper. What I saw caused me to groan inwardly. The top half of the paper was colored green and in bold black letters it proclaimed, "CALIFORNIA FILM CREW PICKS UP 25 OF OUR FINEST AND ONLY BRINGS BACK 24."

I had an appointment that morning with a man who had said he wanted to invest in my film project. As I hailed a taxi and went to his office, I was nearly fainting from exhaustion from the last week of filming. I put on the best face I could and went into his office. When he asked how I was doing, I replied, "Fine!"

"Fine?" he fired back. "Didn't you see the morning paper?" I said I had and it was a tragedy about the man who drowned, but it was done, and all we could do was to move on and finish the project. I pointed out that we were not the first film crew to have ever lost a member of a cast or crew. But he was firm; he didn't want any part of my project. As I left his office, I glanced up on the wall of the waiting room and I saw framed there a quote from Teddy Roosevelt, the twenty-sixth president of the United States:

> It is not the critic who counts; not the man who points out how the strong man stumbles, or where the doer of deeds could have done them better. The credit belongs to the man who is actually in the arena, whose face is marred by dust and sweat and blood; who strives valiantly; who errs, who comes short again and again, because there is no effort without error and shortcoming; but who does actually strive to do the deeds; who knows great enthusiasms, the great devotions; who spends himself in a worthy cause; who at the best knows in the end the triumph of high achievement, and who at the worst, if he fails, at least fails while daring greatly, so that his place shall never be with those cold and timid souls who neither know victory nor defeat.

His quote brought tears to my eyes because I was certainly in the arena, and I was certainly covered by dust and sweat and the blood of the drowned man. And while I certainly seemed to be losing at that moment, I was at least losing while daring greatly. It gave me a tremendous boost at a moment when I needed a boost.

THE OPPORTUNITY IN EVERY MOMENT

I went back to the hotel and realized I had to deal with the hotel owner. I went to him and described my circumstances.

Of course, he had already seen the headlines that morning. He understood that nonpayment of a hotel bill that had now grown to $20,000 would look bad on a month-end profit-and-loss statement and that an investment in a film project would look much better. We, too, came to want the same thing—continuing progress for the film. He chose to regard the situation as a possible lucky break rather than a business problem. It was a bright ray in the midst of my difficulties.

There was one other bright ray. Before I left California, I had arranged for the use of a 120-car freight train in New Orleans. It was to take the cast and crew on their continuing journey across the country as part of the film's story, and we were to begin filming the freight train scenes that afternoon. After I left the hotel owner's office and went back to my room to pack, I was in an improved frame of mind. But I arrived at my room just in time to get a call from the president of the railroad, who was calling to cancel the 120-car freight train. He said that he had read about the drowning in the morning paper and he was sorry, but his railroad had to avoid that kind of publicity.

Being in New Orleans with twelve dollars, the credit cards bursting their limits, a hungry cast and crew, almost all the film used up, two thousand more miles to go, a police investigation of the drowning, and now the loss of the freight train—that was really disheartening. I freely admit to you that my heart sank and sank. What was I to do? I felt lost, alone, deserted, and in incredibly bad circumstances. I was in way over my head and the forces seemed overwhelmingly powerful—and against me.

"But you gave your word!" I shouted at the president of the railroad on the other end of the phone.

"I'm sorry," he said, "my decision is final." I hung up the phone and stared gloomily out of the window.

At moments like those my mind would turn to inquiring of the Universe, "Why? Why me? Why now? Why so bad? Why so hard?"

The answers have evolved over the years: *"For your growth, for your learning, for your understanding, for your strength, for your total and complete benefit."*

I had earlier called the Louisiana film commission and alerted them to the police investigation. They made some calls and the affair was dropped, although I would have to deal with a civil suit.

The hotel owner, as a final gesture of good will, packed us all a lunch and gave us his best wishes. I gathered the cast and the thirty-five crew members together and told them that I had seen a big freight yard on the outskirts of town, and I thought that we all had better go down there since we very much needed a freight train.

It was mid-morning when we arrived at the freight yard. I went into the main freight office and asked the superintendent, whose name was Sam, if it would be all right if we boarded one of his trains and filmed a traveling sequence. I told him I was out of money and couldn't pay for it. He said that he would have to call Kansas City to ask for permission. As he was talking on the phone, I saw him repeatedly looking over at me. When he finished his conversation, he came back to me.

"Are you the guy that lost the man in the Mississippi?" he asked in a rather tough way.

"That's what the newspapers say."

"Well, my boss told me to get you off this lot as fast as I can!"

"Well, I certainly appreciate your effort on our behalf."

"Yeah, it's too bad," he said a little sadly. "I've been waiting twenty-five years to get my train in a film."

Twenty-five years, I thought to myself. *Perhaps we can both have what we want*. I wanted to film the train; he wanted the train to be filmed. We could both have it our way. As I described what I saw as our opportunity, he slowly understood. He realized that this was probably the only chance of fulfilling his dream of twenty-five years. At first, he only let me photograph the outside of the train. He had reasoned it out in his mind that as long as we stayed away from the train, everyone would be safe. Then he looked on as the cast was having their makeup put on, which bystanders always enjoyed watching because they got to see a magical change take place right before their eyes. Sam could see that what I wanted was not hurting his company. He also saw that he could be part of the project through his train. Sam started to become really excited about having his train in a movie after waiting all those years. He and I got to talking about trains and the magic of them.

"Sam," I said, "there are some people who have never been on a train. There are some kids who have only seen pictures of them, who will never get to experience that wonderful feeling of sitting in a boxcar listening to the hollow sound it makes as it goes over a bridge, the clack-clack of the wheels on the rails, who will never get to sit in the open doorway of a boxcar as it rumbles through towns or wave to the people in automobiles waiting for the train to go by, who will never get to see the magic of the moon skipping in and out behind the trees as the engine whistles its eerie way through the countryside. You know, Sam, this is a magical film and it's important that the people who see it know that they're looking at the real thing. I'd like to get on your train when it leaves here in an hour and ride it all the way through Louisiana, filming and recording as we go."

"No siree! Absolutely not! If you got caught, we'd all lose our jobs, for sure."

"Do people still hop freights?"

"Sure they do, but not if we catch them!"

"Well, just take a l-o-n-g, s-l-o-w turn around, and by the time you're facing our direction again, we'll be gone!"

He pondered deeply and slowly said, "Nope, I just can't do it."

I put my hand on his shoulder, looked him in the eye, and said, "Sam, you can do it." For the next ten hours, we filmed some of the most beautiful and exciting footage imaginable as the train swept us along from the mouth of the Mississippi up through Louisiana.

I could have worried myself with questions such as "What if Sam won't let me on his train?" or "What if we get caught and Sam loses his job?" Do not distress yourself with questions like that. When you start on the "what if" questions, they go on forever. Okay, so what if we had gotten caught and Sam lost his job, but then he got another one that was twice as good? What if we had gotten caught and Sam lost his job, and the following week, when Sam would have normally been working on the train, it got into a wreck and all on board were killed—but because Sam lost his job, his life was saved? In the world of "what if," the questions and answers are endless. It is hard enough to deal with reality, with what actually happens, without also trying to deal with the "what ifs" of the world.

As a result of that turning point in the freight yard, I was eventually able to make it all the way across the country to Big Sur, California. Then I spent a year editing the film and finished it in 1976. I finally had the film I wanted.

I learned three very important things during that long odyssey: (1) Never give up on your commitment. (2) The Universe will help when there is nothing left you can possibly do. (3) All of life is a grand adventure when you learn to see it that way. What that story, what every incident in my life, in your life, comes down to is this: *I am the center of my Universe; you are the center of your Universe. I determine what happens for me; you determine what happens for you.*

OUT THERE

Up to this moment, you've created many of the events in the world around you, sometimes knowingly, sometimes unknowingly. It's true that events are being created around you by outside forces—a rainfall, for instance—but it's also true that you are creating events and situations. You are always using your power to create and influence events. You're like a radio station that constantly transmits. Whatever you broadcast goes out over the airwaves in every direction, affecting everyone and everything around you. If you're broadcasting fear, fear is projected to everything around you, and your fear brings to you those things that are attracted by fear. If you're broadcasting power and confidence, everything and everyone around you is affected positively, and you draw to yourself the things that are attracted by power and confidence.

Here's a simple story that illustrates that powerful truth. A man in the Midwest owned a financially successful sandwich shop. It was a small shop, and there were nearly always people in line to buy his products. He put exceptionally generous portions in all of his sandwiches, and he gave away free pickles, free potato chips, and sometimes a free soft drink. One day, his son from New York came to visit him for the first time in several years. He stayed a few days, and as he was preparing to leave he said he thought his dad was making a big mistake putting such huge portions in all his sandwiches and giving away all those extras.

"The country's economy is in bad shape," his son said. "People are out of work, and there is less money to spend. Unless you cut back on the free items and generous portions, you, too, will soon be in a bad way."

The son left and went home to his distant city. The father started thinking about what his son had said, and he decided to follow his son's advice. He stopped giving away free items and he cut down on the generous portions of food he put in his sandwiches. Soon afterwards, when many of his disappointed customers stopped coming, he wrote to his son, "You're right, son! The country's economy is in bad shape and I'm experiencing the results of it right here in my sandwich shop!"

The poor economy this man's son saw all around him was real. However, in the midst of the poor economy, his father was running a successful sandwich shop. He had been unaware that times were hard, that many people were out of work, that money was scarce. When he heard about it from his son, he began to act as if it were so and brought about the only possible result, a negative, fearful, ungenerous experience of life—an experience he believed to be "out there."

Was it really "out there?" Who cut back on the portions of food? Who eliminated the give-away items? Who was it that made the first move? You know the answer.

How about your own life? Who is responsible for the areas in your life that you are dissatisfied with? It's harder to see the answer to that in your own life because you've been thinking for so long that you're only reacting to what's "out there." Yet what's really happening is that what's "out there" is reacting to you.

EXERCISE NUMBER ONE

"I Am the Center of My Personal Universe"

Memorize the statement *"I am the center of my personal Universe."* As you did in the earlier exercise, write down this statement on several pieces of paper, carry it with you, and put it where you will see it—on your bathroom mirror, on the dashboard of your car if you drive, on the ceiling above your bed, on your wallet. Allow this truth to live in your consciousness. It is powerful information that will greatly benefit you. Keep those papers around until this concept is thoroughly embedded in your consciousness.

A major purpose of this program is to increase your awareness that you are the center of your personal Universe, influencing everyone and everything around you. This exercise is designed to keep you more aware for more minutes of every day that you are affecting everyone and everything around you by being "Who You Are."

EXERCISE NUMBER TWO

Acting with the Knowledge That All Events Are for Your Benefit

To carry forward the exercise in chapter 5, continue viewing the events in your life with this concept in mind: *The Universe is causing every event that occurs in my life so that I can be benefited in the maximum amount possible.*

You may have to continue to stretch your imagination for this, but imagine that everything the Universe brings about—whether it's rain, sunshine, automobile accidents, blooming flowers, a stubbed toe, and even such trivia as a torn cuticle—is all for your total and complete benefit. If you wake up in the morning and it's a foggy day, look out the window and say, "The Universe has ordered this wonderful foggy morning particularly for me for some wonderful reason I am not yet aware of." Act *as if* the Universe is responsible for creating the mist that you are beholding. Treat that weather as though the Universe had ordered the most beneficial weather possible for you. Make believe, if you have to, that this weather is exactly suited to your particular needs of that day.

Of course, the next time you plan a Sunday outing or picnic and you wake up and it's raining, you will have your work cut out for you. However, that's when this exercise becomes most important and most relevant. Your job is to act as though the rainy day is the most beneficial condition that could happen for you at that moment. You may discover later that the area you had chosen for the outing was the scene of a bad accident or a riot that day or that because you stayed home, an important event in your life took place that caused you to bless that rainy morning that kept you inside. After you have enough "rainy-day experiences" that turn out perfectly, you'll have no difficulty believing that everything occurs for your total and complete benefit. One of the key benefits to adopting this perspective is that it keeps you feeling good no matter what happens around you.

What's important is to keep on practicing. Practice being grateful for the rainy day or the foggy morning. Practice treating it as though the Universe created it for you. Practice thinking of every event as the best event possible. Like everything else, the more you do it, the more expert you become at doing it. If a person greets you cheerfully, take it upon yourself to believe that the Universe, which is taking care of you every moment, caused it. If a person greets you with irritation or treats you with less respect, consideration, or love than you believe you deserve, say to yourself: *"The Universe created this response for me. It's the most beneficial response I could experience. I can change the way this person is responding to me by making a change in myself, which that person will then react to in a better way."* Once you have decided what the change should be, make it. It may take you a while to know which inner changes will bring about the desired results, but with practice you'll soon find out.

Thinking that the Universe is the sole cause of all that happens, and also that everything that happens is for your benefit, is hard. But the hardest part, by far, is giving up acting the part of a powerless person. That involves giving up the self-defeating comfort of blaming bad luck for seeming failures. There is no such thing as bad luck. What seems like bad luck is only good fortune clothed in a disguise. One of the main reasons there are so few truly happy people in the world is due to faulty perception, not to bad luck. When you treat the event as bad luck, you give it the power to be bad. You can change that.

The effort you put into this exercise will yield life-changing results. The reward for being successful in this undertaking will be right up there with the greatest results you have ever experienced up to this point in your life, nearly as life-changing as the realization that the Universe is alive, conscious, and aware—totally aware of you. If you have not experienced that yet, go back and read the first part of the book again.

EXERCISE NUMBER THREE

Describing Your Hopes

At the end of this exercise is a page with the heading "My Hopes." On that page, write down what you hope for yourself. Search your mind. Let your imagination roam. Think about what you truly want for yourself. Then, regardless of how seemingly difficult or far-fetched the object of your desire is, write it down.

Be as descriptive as you can in writing what your hopes are. If, for instance, you want to take a trip around the world, describe it in as much detail as possible. If you hope for a mate or a friend, describe what you hope he or she will be like. If you hope to obtain a possession of some kind, describe it as completely as you can.

Be optimistic and realistic in your hopes and practical in obtaining them. If you want to become a great singer, for example, but have had no training and don't have much of a voice, be sure you visualize yourself taking singing lessons as part of your hope to reach your goal. The Universe usually does not just drop an unearned gift in your lap.

What you hope for is what will draw you along the path to your evolution as a great person. Do not delude yourself into thinking that your goals are the end-all and be-all of life; they merely lead you on the path. It is the path to the attainment of your goals that is the end-all and be-all of life, for that is where strength and wisdom are gained and where happiness unfolds.

Be sure the hopes you write down are personal. They should be your hopes for yourself. "I hope my son is financially successful" or "I hope my son finds happiness" is not in line with what is intended for this exercise. Your hopes are to be for you alone, although they might include someone else, such as hoping to find a mate or a friend for yourself. You may list any number of hopes, whether many or only a few. Then sign your name on the line provided and write the date.

As you progress through this program, you may find that your hopes change. If that happens, change your list of hopes. You may add to your list or cross off hopes you no longer desire. When a hope is fulfilled, simply write "fulfilled" next to it. If you run out of room on the pages provided, get a piece of paper, cut it to the size of the page in the book, and write neatly across the top of the page "My Hopes." Then tape it into the book with double-sided cellophane tape or glue the page at its edge into the book.

Keep all the papers you write on as part of this exercise, even if what you write on some of the papers becomes completely crossed out because you have made changes or fulfilled hopes. When drawing a line through a hope, use only one light line so that what you originally wrote will still be readable.

Give this exercise plenty of thought, for you are now going to take a critically important step in bringing about what you want—*imagining it*. Each time you begin a new chapter, review your hopes list and visualize those hopes becoming realities. See yourself attaining them.

My Hopes:

Signature:____________________________________ **Date:**____________

My Hopes:

Signature:______________________________ **Date:**__________

EXERCISE NUMBER FOUR

Learning to Be Happy—Pleasure Exercise #5

Enjoy another half hour of pleasure. Begin by saying, *"I, [say your name], give myself permission to enjoy a half hour of pleasure."*

Fulfill this exercise by yourself. You may spend your half hour where there are other people, but do not take anyone with you or arrange to meet anyone. If you meet someone by chance, that's fine. Remember, at the end of the half hour, if the time you spent was less than pleasurable, start over or choose another pleasure exercise.

After you have completed this exercise, write a brief summary on the next page under the heading "Pleasure Exercise #5" along with the date you completed it.

Complete the exercises in this chapter before going on to chapter 7.

Pleasure Exercise #5:

Date completed: ______________________________

7

YOUR PERSONAL UNIVERSE

There is no reality except the one contained within us.
That is why so many people live such an unreal life. They
take the images outside them for reality and never
allow the world within to assert itself.
—Hermann Hesse

HOW FAR CAN YOU SEE? Put this book down for a moment and answer that question.

I have heard many answers. Some people say, "Whatever the distance is to the farthest object" or "As far as the skyline." Others say, "It depends on the day." Still others say they can see the sun, which is 93 million miles away, or they can see the stars, which are trillions of miles away.

In reality, you don't see far at all. Actually, you don't see "out" at all. The only thing you see are light rays as they enter your eyes after being radiated from or reflected off an object. Your eyes are receivers. We do not see objects; we see the light rays that bounce off the objects. When light enters your eye, it first passes through the cornea, then the pupil, the lens, the aqueous humor, and the vitreous humor until it reaches the retina, which is the light-sensing structure of the eye. The retina contains cells called rods and cones, so named because of their shape. Rods handle vision in low light, provide peripheral vision, and detect motion, and cones handle color vision and detail. The retina contains approximately 100 to 120 million rods and approximately 6 to 7 million cones.

The rays of light that enter your eye stimulate these rods and cones and, in turn, create electrical impulses that travel along the optic nerve system to the brain. The brain, in an incredibly complex manner, receives those impulses and forms a picture. Where do you think the picture is? Is it "out there," in front of your eyes, as it appears to be? The picture, in fact, is totally inside your head. It is formed by your brain within your brain according to the electrical impulses it received and its own hardware and software.

Think about what the explanation of this picture-making process means to you. Think about how that changes your relationship to the "outside" world. Do you realize that in your entire lifetime you have never actually seen an "object"? The only things you have ever seen were light rays being radiated by or reflected from objects. Every rock, every tree, every person, every house, every car, everything you have ever seen, or thought you saw, including yourself, was just light rays that assembled a picture inside your head when those light rays bounced off the objects and entered your eyes. The view you have of the world is simply a picture that *appears* to be outside but is actually *totally inside* your head.

EVERYTHING IS DIFFERENT FROM EVERYTHING ELSE

Are the images you see the same images that everyone else sees? There are no two spider webs alike, no two blades of grass alike, no two snowflakes alike, no two leaves alike, no two stars alike, no two hairs alike, no two cells alike, no two rocks alike—no two anything alike. The differentiation is *total; everything* is different from everything else. Since all those things are different, can you imagine that the 100 million rods and 7 million cones in your eyes are different from the 100 million rods and 7 million cones that are in every other person's eyes? Even if only a few of the rods and cones were different, you would still form pictures that were slightly different from everyone else's pictures.

Beyond the mechanical process of seeing, there are other differences that make what you see different from what everyone else sees. When we form inner pictures, we react to those pictures based upon our past experiences. One woman sees the color red and thinks of a beautiful rose given to her a long time ago, reminding her of a great love. Another woman sees the same shade of red and remembers the matador's red cape and how shocked and horrified she was when the bull was killed, its red blood running down its side—the same shade of red as the matador's cape. The two women react to the same color in extremely different ways.

If ten people were sitting in a circle around a small pond with the moon nearly overhead and all ten pointed to the reflection they saw of the moon on the pond, every person would point to a different place, depending on where he or she was sitting. Yet all of them would think that they were looking at the same reflection.

Of course, there are also differences in how we perceive things through our other senses. Part of the human equipment you use to hear is a tightly stretched membrane known as the eardrum. It is smaller than your pinky nail and much thinner, and it works just like a drum. Sound vibrations hit the drum and those vibrations are transmitted to the three smallest bones in your body known as the hammer, anvil, and stirrup, so called because those bones resemble those objects. The bones vibrate to the sensations they receive and the vibrations are, in turn, passed along through a coiled tube called the cochlea, which has thousands of tiny hairs in it called cilia. The hairs vibrate and electrical impulses are sent along the auditory nerve to your brain, where the sensations are interpreted.

You can imagine that all your hearing equipment is different from everyone else's hearing equipment. Some people have keener hearing than others. Some people can hear higher-pitched sounds than others. Similarly, your senses of touch, taste, and smell are different from everyone else's. *Everything* is different for every person. The difference may be only slight, but it's that slight difference that makes all the difference.

One day I was talking to a group of twelve people, and I picked up a toy figure of a Pink Panther made of some plastic material that could be formed into different positions, and I put it into a standing position with its arms upraised. I then asked the twelve people in the room what they thought the Pink Panther was doing. One said he was praying, one said he was stretching, one said he was dancing, and another said he was singing. Each person saw the Pink Panther doing something different. One person even imagined that he was holding a rock above his head.

It is like that with all events in life. Each person sees them differently, reacts to them differently, and therefore causes different results to occur because of how each one reacts to and interprets what he or she saw. One person sees an event as a loss; another sees the same event as a gain or an opportunity.

What does all this mean to you? It means that everything you see, hear, touch, smell, taste, or experience in any way is different for you than it is for anyone else. It means that you have to rely solely and completely on what's true for you. If you rely on what's true for another, you'll probably be slightly off course.

YOU CREATE THE RESULTS

Many years ago, I was training a small group of salespeople to use the same principles that are in this book. One of the salespeople, Walter, took to the teaching immediately. He quickly grasped the ideas behind the principles and was quite excited by what he was learning. During the training, the following incident occurred, and it gave him an opportunity to put what he was learning into action. Another member of the sales team, James, had listed a house for sale and Walter sold the house to one of his clients. The house was in a very rough part of town, where several tough gangs regularly vandalized houses. So to protect the house until the escrow closed, the company hired a night watchman to look after the property. The very first night, one of the gangs beat up the night watchman and vandalized the house with a lot of graffiti.

The next morning, when the salesmen heard about it, James said, "Well, that's the end of that sale. The buyer will never buy the house now."

"That's what you think!" said Walter. "Do you mind if I call your seller?" James agreed.

"Listen to this," said Walter. He picked up the phone and called the seller and told him what had happened. He told the seller that unless he could get a price reduction, the sale would be lost. The seller agreed to a five-thousand-dollar price reduction.

Walter then called the buyer and said, "I have some great news for you!" He told the buyer what had transpired the night before and then said, "And I used that incident to get you a five-thousand-dollar price reduction!" The buyer, who knew it was a rough neighborhood, was delighted and thanked the quick-thinking salesman profusely. One of those men saw the incident as a piece of bad luck that would ruin his sale, and the other saw it as an opportunity to make the sale more firm. One used the event to envision failure, and the other used it to envision success.

Walter used a Universal principle you've been learning about in this book—the principle that says that how we respond to an event determines its outcome—and he used it perfectly to ensure success. That day he was only using it so he and his friend could make a sale, but I knew he would go on to use the same principle in a much bigger arena, perhaps to purchase the house that everyone says is not for sale or to invent a new machine that everyone says cannot be invented. That attitude, that "inner knowing," when fully developed, will be "what's true for Walter," and it will carry him to the fulfillment of his dreams and a wonderfully satisfying life, having things the way he wants them.

In every situation, there are generally two basic options open to you. James's attitude when he and Walter first heard about the vandalism of the house demonstrates exactly where one of those options will lead—directly to failure. He said,

"That's the end of that sale." He was hurrying to failure. Walter's response—"That's what you think—listen to this!"—is the kind of response that leads directly to success.

This is much more than a simple situation with an unusual salesperson. Walter actually created the result! Take a moment to think about this. Walter created his future in a special way. The same pieces of reality were there for both men: the house, the night watchman who was hurt, the vandalism, and the buyer and seller of the house. James used them in the way he usually used the pieces of reality he perceived—he was ready and willing to accept less than he wanted. Walter, however, saw the situation differently. With the new way of looking at things that he had learned at the sales lessons, he created a success, which then reinforced his belief that he can have things just the way he wants them. Now it's your turn.

Here's the heart of this concept: *You participate, moment by moment, in the creation of your Universe*. It's an easy concept to understand but a difficult one to keep aware of as you participate in your everyday life. When you believe you can do something, you create the stream of events that brings about what you believe. What you fail to believe you can do, you fail to bring about. Henry Ford, the auto manufacturer, said it best: "Whether you think you can or you can't, you're right!"

BREAKING THROUGH THE SHELL OF RESTRICTED THINKING

I was waiting at a small airport many years ago, when I struck up a conversation with one of the airport workers, a young man of about twenty. During our talk he found out I had a private pilot's license, and he said that he would love to get his pilot's license. I asked him why he was waiting.

"It's too expensive," he said. "As soon as I found out how much the lessons cost, I gave up the idea."

"There's opportunity all around you," I responded energetically. "You work at an airport! Talk to the owners of the planes, talk to the pilots, talk to the crew members, find out if there's something you can do in exchange for lessons. When you decide you can't do it, it's over. You can just as easily decide to do it and, in time, you'll have your pilot's license!"

He shrugged his shoulders, looked at me as if I were a little strange, and said, "Nope, I don't think so. It's too expensive. When I heard how much it cost, I just turned away from it."

"But you're turning away from life, from yourself, from opportunity, and you're acting as if you're powerless! Are you powerless?"

He shrugged his shoulders, laughed a little, looked at me again as if I were strange, and walked away.

This young man was faced with the same two choices we are all faced with at varying times in our lives. You can either take positive action to bring about what you want or you can shrug your shoulders and walk away. Your success or failure is foretold by your actions, by what you believe. For a limitation to be valid, *you must accept it*. Start believing that you are a special person who has the ability to do what you want to do. Act on that belief! It is a difficult task—to break out of a shell of restricted thinking and into your perfect personal Universe of expanded thinking—but you can do it!

Until recently, you've lived your life believing that having what you want is limited, so your actions were based on that belief. Consequently, you produced results consistent with your belief. Your belief was then reinforced by the "reality" you created. Now, who created the "reality"?

It is important that you fully understand what it means to "produce results consistent with your belief." If you believe you can do something, you will act based on that belief. If you believe something is impossible to do, you will fail to even begin. Your action or inaction will bring about results consistent with what you decide.

Read the next paragraph aloud, as though you had written it:

> *This is my time to have the circumstances of my life the way I want them. All-That-Is responds to me. In the midst of the always-unfolding Universal events, I participate in directing and controlling the outcome of events in my personal Universe. I participate in creating the circumstances of my life, moment by moment. To change those outward circumstances, I make changes in myself. I affect All-That-Is by being "Who I Am" at every moment. I am a pure, bright spirit—a perfect being. I act with that knowledge and the Universe responds in the only way possible—with what I want.*

YOU CAN DANCE IF YOU WANT TO

You can already feel new awareness and capability within you, but perhaps you're still uncertain how far it extends. It extends to the height, width, and depth of your personal Universe. In that Universe, the most basic, most important law is "cause and effect" and the most important element is you because you are causing the effects by how you are being at every moment.

In one of my Power Workshops, there was a young man, Zachary, who had gone to discos for many years to watch people dance. He yearned to dance with the girls, but he could only stand on the sidelines, watching, because the thought of walking across the dance floor and asking one of them to dance was too frightening. The image of being rejected and then having to make that long, embarrassing walk back again, with everyone knowing what had happened, was more than he could bear. His fear of it was so intense that he would sweat just thinking about it. Sometimes there seems to be no reasonable explanation for the fear within us. It's nothing to be ashamed of; it's just there and must be dealt with. *Fortunately, we have enough courage to overcome even our worst fear.*

The years passed and Zachary's longing grew. He would dance at home with his radio playing, and he was a really good dancer, but that only made matters worse in his mind. Being a good dancer and not being able to dance with a girl seemed to compound the problem.

If you could have seen Zachary and heard his sad tale, you would have chuckled, as I did, for he was a fine-looking young man, about six feet tall with broad shoulders, a fair suntanned complexion, and smooth, even features. He looked the image of a California surfer. It seemed as if any woman would be pleased to dance with him. But what lived inside of Zachary was a scared little boy who was terrified of rejection.

One Friday evening, after he had been in the workshop about two weeks, Zachary went to his favorite disco and took up his accustomed place against the wall. Suddenly, he remembered that he was attending a Power Workshop, that this was a workout situation, and that the outcome, whatever it was, would completely benefit him. He brought to mind his perfect image and, with his heart thudding in his chest and at a loss for breath, he walked across the dance floor to the woman he was most attracted to and invited her to dance. She was delighted.

That night, Zachary danced every dance and with any woman he chose. The following Monday evening at the workshop, he was so proud of himself and so filled with happiness and certainty that he told us he believed he could do anything. He told us that he was moving out of his parents' house, that he was going to get a new wardrobe, and that he was going to start a band. He talked about his new plans and ideas and told us he was certain that he could fulfill all of them.

The courage and the strength to do all of that had always been within Zachary; he had only to call upon it. It's the very same courage and strength that is within you. You may not believe you have that courage and strength, but you do, and they are waiting on the sidelines of your mind, just waiting for you to say the words that will bring them forth. And those words are "Let's do it!"

At the start of the twenty-first century, one of the greatest truths of our time is that you are the master maker and molder of your personal Universe. As you believe, so it is for you.

What do you want? What changes would you like to make? Now is the time to make them. At this instant, you can make the decision to bring about what you want. Because "now" is a continually unfolding event, your decision must always live within you, and you must continually reinforce that decision whenever it comes to mind. When a decision you make lives within you, it always influences your actions and it will eventually bring you to the achievement of your goals. It's your ever-present willpower directed toward a precise outcome that will lead you unerringly to the attainment of what you desire.

Give in to your wholesome desires! Allow yourself to be drawn toward your goals. Hold your goals lightly in your mind, taking every opportunity that comes along to move in the direction of your goals. Believe that you will arrive at those goals safely and happily. As you travel through life, remember that the Universal law of cause and effect is absolute. What you experience will be a reflection of what you put out there. By acting knowledgeably and treating each incident as "just right for you," everything in your personal Universe will reflect your positive actions.

Pause for a moment. Think what it means to have your entire personal Universe reflect your actions. Treat yourself well by being the best person you know how to be. You can dance if you want to!

EXERCISE NUMBER ONE

Switching Past Events to a Positive Track

Find a place where you can sit comfortably and quietly, free from interruption. Close your eyes and mentally go back to your childhood and then come forward by separating your life into blocks of time, such as preschool, early school, summer vacations, trips, moving from one home to another, different ages, memorable events, different jobs. As you remember your way forward from childhood, remember the events that seemed hurtful to you because of things that others did to you. Those events can reflect any kind of hurt—physical, financial, moral, or emotional.

One by one, review each incident in as much detail as you can, and then carefully switch it onto a positive track. See the incident as beneficial in every way. Think of the extra-nice events that have occurred since that hurtful event took place. As you've been practicing in earlier exercises, realize that those hurtful events were just events that you needed in order to gain the information, wisdom, or experience that would someday prove valuable in leading you to happier events. Realize that the hurtful event was an essential part of a sequence of events that brought about that later, happier event.

Use the good events as leverage to help put the hurtful event onto a positive track. Even though you will see the first event as hurtful when it first comes to mind, call it beneficial. Say it's good without believing it if you need to. Stay with it until the hurt is gone and you've freed yourself from the burden of carrying a hurt from your past.

Just as it's nice to live in a clean home, wear clean clothes, and be clean yourself, it's nice to have a clean past. It provides you with a happy now and expectations for a bright future. Stay with this exercise until it's done. It would almost be better for you to remain seated forever than to get up carrying around all that extra baggage from the past. It clutters up now. You have far too much to do in your future to permit your past to slow you down. To be happy today, you need to rid yourself of past hurts.

All that happens—now, then, sooner, or later—happens for your greatest benefit. Allow that knowledge to live in your consciousness and you will always live in "the world of perfect," handling new events in a way that leaves you whole, in charge, feeling good, and grateful for the event's occurrence.

Accomplish this exercise in two sessions of a half hour each. Leave at least a two-hour period between the two sessions. A half hour is the least amount of time you should spend in each session. You may take as many sessions as you need in order to accomplish your exercise, but for the purpose of going on to the next chapter, you may consider this exercise completed after accomplishing two half-hour sessions.

EXERCISE NUMBER TWO

Changing Your Perception of Missed Opportunities

I heard an interview years ago with a famous man in his eighties who said, "I only regret the things I *didn't* do."

We all have regrets about things that we didn't do that we wish we had done. It seems as if it's part of human nature to have those regrets, but it's actually a learned response that no longer benefits us. The following exercise will be of great benefit in reorganizing your thought patterns to relieve you of those unpleasant memories from the past. It will also help you create a beneficial response to future events.

Think of at least three missed opportunities in your life that you wish you had not missed. Think about those missed opportunities in as much detail as you can. Live those feelings of having missed those opportunities. Now change those feelings into good feelings, knowing that those missed opportunities were perfect *for you*.

This is a powerful exercise and of critical importance in being who you want and having what you want. Do not let negative feelings about missed opportunities engulf you any longer. First of all, you were supposed to miss them, and, secondly, the information you gained from missing the opportunity was far more important to you than taking the opportunity would have been. Do not go forward until you have freed yourself from any negative thoughts you hold about your missed opportunities. You may remember more than three missed opportunities. If that's the case, do the same for all of them.

EXERCISE NUMBER THREE

Learning to Be Happy—Pleasure Exercise #6

Give yourself permission to create and experience a half hour of pleasure. Begin by saying, *"I, [say your name], give myself permission to experience a half hour of pleasure."*

Before selecting your new pleasure exercise, read each of your summaries for the previous five pleasure exercises. This time, push your boundaries out a bit to experience more of the pleasure life has to offer.

Fulfill this exercise with another person. Tell the person it's an exercise in a program you're following. If the experience turns out to be less than pleasurable, start over or choose another exercise or another person.

After the exercise is completed, write a brief summary on the next page under the heading "Pleasure Exercise #6" and write the date you completed the exercise.

Complete the exercises in this chapter before going on to chapter 8.

Pleasure Exercise #6

Date completed: ______________________________

8

POSSIBILITIES

If I were to wish for anything, I should not wish for wealth and power, but for the passionate sense of the potential, for the eye which, ever young and ardent, sees the possible.
—Sören Kierkegaarde

BY NOW, YOU HAVE SEEN THE UNIVERSE RESPOND to your new way of being, which has increased your confidence in yourself. It is now time to shake off still more of the beliefs you've accepted that are preventing you from being who you want and having what you want. Deep in your innermost mental recesses should live the belief *"All things are possible for me because I believe that all things are possible."* That truth is a precious jewel in your treasure chest of knowledge. You've got to know in your heart "I can do it." Do what? *Anything!*

One evening, as I started a Power Workshop, I asked everyone in the room what they would most like to do if they had all the power they wanted. In reply to this question, a tall, handsome, rugged-looking man named Patrick looked at me and said, "I'm in the Ironworkers' Union and if I had all the power I wanted, I'd want to work on the bridge."

"The bridge?" I asked. "What bridge?"

"What do you mean, what bridge?" he replied indignantly. "There's only one bridge—Golden Gate!"

"The Golden Gate Bridge is in San Francisco. If you want to work on that bridge, then what are you doing in Los Angeles?"

"It's not that easy," he said forcefully. "You can't just go work on 'The Bridge'!"

"Why not?"

"Are you kidding?" he replied in an unbelieving tone. "First you've got to win your suspenders and your hard hat. They only take the best up there!"

"What do you mean 'you've got to win your suspenders and your hard hat'? Don't you have those things?"

He looked at me as if I really didn't know anything at all and replied, "Those are levels of ironworking, grades of expertise. It's more than that, though. Even when you've reached those levels, you've got to know somebody. That bridge is run by a union, a tough union!" Then, he added reverently, as though he were in church and speaking about God, "It's the Ironworkers' Union."

"Oh, so does that mean that you can't work on the bridge?"

"Of course that's what it means!"

After a long pause, I asked, "Can you see that it's *your belief* in the way things are that prevents you from going to San Francisco and getting a job on the bridge?"

"It's not my belief that keeps me from going to San Francisco; it's the union!"

"Oh, the union! What would you say if I told you I could go to San Francisco and get a job working on the bridge and I'm not even a union member—or an ironworker?"

He laughed uproariously at that and began to ridicule me, saying, "You? They wouldn't let you within a mile of that bridge! Do you know how dangerous that work is? Do you think they're going to risk their jobs and all that liability by allowing you to work on the bridge? You must be crazy! Huh! That's the stupidest thing I've ever heard!"

"Patrick, suppose I went to the people in charge of hiring for the Golden Gate Bridge and told them I was writing a book about the greatest bridge in the world and the men who work on it and that to gather information, I wanted to work on the bridge for a day. What do you think they'd say?"

"What do I think they'd say? I *know* what they'd say. They'd get you away from that bridge quicker than you could bat an eyelash! You don't know how dangerous that work is! They would *never* let you work on the bridge."

"Well, Patrick, what if I went to the foreman of the bridge and told him that one of his fellow ironworkers, a man named Patrick, had given up his will to live as a great human being, a great ironworker. Suppose I told him that Patrick no longer believed in himself, but he had one great desire and that was to work on the greatest bridge in America, the Golden Gate. Suppose I told the foreman that Patrick had lost so much confidence in himself that he despaired of ever being able to reach that goal. Suppose I told him that if I could get to work on the bridge, even for one day, it might inspire Patrick enough and give him enough courage to continue on as the truly great man and ironworker he really is. Now, Patrick, what do you think he'd say to that?"

Patrick threw back his head and laughed. "I think that is the biggest load of garbage I've ever heard!"

"Okay, Patrick. Because you believe that you have to first

win your suspenders and your hard hat and know somebody in the union in order to get to work on the bridge, you have convinced yourself that you can't get a job working on the bridge and that you might just as well remain here in Los Angeles rather than go to San Francisco to try to get a job working on the bridge. You are rooted here in Los Angeles *by your belief*. If I believe what you tell me, that it's impossible for me to get a job on the bridge, I also have to remain here in Los Angeles without ever going to San Francisco to even attempt to get a job working on the bridge. On the other hand, if I believe that all things are possible *for those who believe that all things are possible*, I can go to San Francisco and, one way or another, I'll get to work on the bridge."

"Look," he said, "I'm getting kind of mad. I don't want to hear any more of this crap!"

He quit the workshop at the end of the first week.

FIGHTING TIDES, OPINIONS, AND LIMITING BELIEFS

In the 1920s, an engineer from Chicago named Joseph Strauss stood at the mouth of the San Francisco Bay, which is called Golden Gate, and said, "I can build a bridge across the entrance to this bay!" Engineers said it was impossible. The press ridiculed the project. Geologists laughed and said that the first earthquake would quickly demolish any bridge across San Francisco's Golden Gate. Strauss and his supporters persisted, and in 1930, although it was one year into the Great Depression, San Francisco citizens overwhelmingly voted in favor of a $35 million bond issue to construct the bridge.

For nearly five years, Joseph Strauss and his builders

fought tides, public opinion, wind, storms, and the ocean itself until they finished what is today one of the most beautiful landmarks in the world. The south tower is 746 feet above water, which is higher than a seventy-story building, and its foundations had to be built 110 feet underwater! The bridge still stands, a monument to the courage, the determination, and the belief of Joseph Strauss.

On one hand, we have Joseph Strauss, the man who engineered and supervised the building of the Golden Gate Bridge. On the other hand, we have Patrick, whose belief system prevented him from getting a job on that wonderful bridge, even though the superhuman feat of building the bridge had been accomplished in great part by ironworkers just like him. More than that, *his belief prevented him from going to San Francisco to even apply for a job on the bridge!*

Patrick said "no" for the foreman of the bridge without ever even talking to him. He said "no" for the Universe, with its endless possibilities. What if Patrick had gone to San Francisco to apply for a job on the bridge just as several key men called in with the flu? What if a new foreman had just started and he wanted several new men to work on the bridge? What if the day Patrick showed up looking for work the foreman had a special need for an exceptionally tall ironworker?

Do you know the difference between Joseph Strauss and our ironworker, Patrick? One believed he could; the other believed he could not. One man had the courage and the belief that he could design and build a bridge across San Francisco's Golden Gate; the other man could not even go to San Francisco to apply for a job on that same bridge. What a vast difference between these two men, and yet they are separated from each other only by what they believed.

Are you holding yourself back from doing something because you believe you can't do it?

BELIEVE IN SOMETHING—AND ACT

At one point during my first attempt at filming *Goin' Home*, I was in Tallahassee, Florida, at a farm where five caretakers lived—five really nice people who were allowed to live there in exchange for looking after the property. The head of the little farm group, Don, was married to a lovely girl, Sandy, and they had a newborn son, Seth. The thirty-five of us who made up the crew and the cast arrived there with our buses, trucks, cars, and expensive equipment, and even though I barely had enough money to sustain us, it looked to them as if we must be wealthy. In contrast, the five on the farm were having a difficult time getting through the winter because in northern Florida the winters can be mighty chilly and they didn't have much money.

One evening shortly after we arrived, Don showed me around the little farmhouse. At one point, he looked at me and his eyes flashed as he pointed to a Bible on the mantle.

"You see that book?" he said. "That's the only book I've read in the last ten years!"

He talked about what a wonderful book it was. He was very powerful in his conviction that his Bible contained all the information and all the guidance he needed and he was very proud of his dedication to it.

A week later, at the end of our filming there, Don invited me to stay and have a final dinner with "the family." It was a warm, friendly gathering.

After dinner Don said wishfully, "If only we could get to Hawaii—I have friends there. You know, in Hawaii my wife and baby and I could stay on the beach! The weather is just perfect. We could live in a tent and eat avocados and mangoes and grapefruit right off the trees! We could live off the land!" He gave a long sigh and shook his head sadly. "It would be marvelous, if only I could get us there."

I asked him why he remained in Florida.

"Ah, shucks," he said. "We don't have any money." He said it with more than a bit of embarrassment.

"Do you need money to get to Hawaii?" I inquired.

"Well, how do you get there?" he asked.

"You get your baby and your wife, you pack up the things you want, and you walk out the door," I answered in a matter-of-fact way. "You figure out where Hawaii is and head for it."

"I know the route and all that. You go to California first. But this is February. What happens if we get to the middle of Texas and run into a snowstorm and we don't get picked up? We have four-month-old Seth. What do we do then?"

"Well, what happens if you go out there, stick out your thumb, and the first person who comes by picks you up and takes you all the way to California?"

"That's a mighty big 'if,'" he said.

"Yeah, but your 'if' keeps you here. My 'if' gets you to California!"

"I don't know, Chris. I hear what you're saying, but I don't think I can take that risk."

"Don, you have very little money and your circumstances here on the farm are very poor. So I suggest you put your Bible to some good use. Tear the pages out of it and use them to start your fires."

"What? Burn my Bible! Are you crazy? That's the word of God! You lookin' for trouble?"

"Come on, Don. If you believed what you read in your Bible, you would go out on the road and put your thumb out and end up on the other side of the country. *That's how a powerful person who has faith acts.* Some people believe in God, some in themselves, some in luck. But the people who are powerful and believe in something *act* on their belief!"

Don was still angry because I had said he had little faith and should burn his Bible, so I said, "I'll tell you what, Don. I'll give you a place to go in Los Angeles, if you ever get enough courage or belief to go."

I wrote down the name and address of a friend who lived there and said, "Somebody is almost always at the house and will welcome you."

I shook hands with everyone and left.

I returned the next morning to say a final good-bye, but Don, Sandy, and Seth were gone. Four days later, I got a call from my friend in Los Angeles, who said, "Don, Sandy, and Seth are here!" They stayed with my friend in California about six weeks while Don worked as a carpenter and then they made their way to Hawaii, where they lived off the land for the winter.

One elemental truth has become clear to me through the years, and it's this: When we undertake a project, if we put out our utmost effort and we come to a point where we have no more effort left within us—and I mean no more—then the Universe will step in and help. It always gives us enough help to get us past the tipping point, where we can then take over again with our own effort and see the project through to completion.

Confucius, a Chinese sage who lived twenty-five hundred years ago, said: "When a person gives up, it is the saddest of all things." He knew that when a person gives up, it's over, but as long as the person keeps on doing his or her best, he or she will succeed. Confucius also said, "When heaven blesses us, it helps us, and to be helped by heaven is to be helped indeed!" The Universe knows exactly what we need to succeed.

NOW IS THE TIME TO DO IT

When you wish to do something, anything, believe that you have the capability to do it. In the beginning, you may have to pretend that's true. However, make your plan and follow it through confidently. Allow yourself to act with the power that is already within you. That power is a perfect and completely capable force that is yours to use as you wish in every situation.

This is a life for doing! This is a life for getting on with it! The only two elements that you ever need to bring about what you want are your belief that it is possible and your will to do it.

Beware of your old conditioning. In earlier years, you learned that many goals were closed to you. You learned that many opportunities were outside of your capabilities. Change those beliefs now! Look at *all* goals as achievable. Don't say "no" for the Universe. Know that you can achieve what you wish to achieve, that you can have what you want to have. Let your imagination roam freely. Look into the wonderful world of total possibility that surrounds you, knowing that your choices are limited *only when you accept the limitations*.

Was there ever a time in your life when an opportunity came along and you failed to take it? Did you ever have the desire to do something "bigger than life"? Is it something you still want to do? Now is your time to do it!

Beginning to do something, even though you are having a hard time seeing how you will be able to finish it, is one of the major steps in accomplishing your heart's desires. It's like seeing a mountain in the distance that you have to cross over in order to get to a place that holds a great treasure. From where you are, it looks as though it's impossible to climb the distant mountain, but your inner belief that you can do it permits you to take the first step and then another. As you get closer and closer to the mountain, you will finally see the small trail that leads up and over the top—the one that was hidden to you until your courage and belief brought you close enough to see it. And I will tell you a secret—*the trail is always there!*

The way to start toward your goal is to take the first step toward it. Take that step believing that you will arrive at your goal. It's that inner belief that brings you to every goal. The real treasure, though, is not in the attainment of the goal but in the traveling. That's where life reveals itself in its moment-by-moment unfolding. That's where wisdom is gained, where your power blossoms, and where happiness is to be found. As your life unfolds, let it find you traveling along, saying with a smile, "Here I am, traveling this wonder-filled path, believing all will be well!" And All-That-Is will respond in the only way it can—by fulfilling your belief.

EXERCISE NUMBER ONE

All Things Are Possible

Have a talk with someone about the possibility that "all things are possible for those who believe that all things *are* possible." Spend fifteen minutes having this conversation. Inform your conversation partner that you want to have this discussion as an exercise in a program you're following. The outcome of the discussion is of little importance. What is of major importance is that you are opening your mind to the possibility that you can have what you want. It's a means of stretching your mind.

Stay away from "prove it" topics like physically floating in air or mentally moving heavy objects. They will only reinforce the limiting concepts you now believe. Instead, discuss the possibility of undertaking what may seem be an almost-impossible task. Take the position that you can do it.

If the person you're talking to disagrees, which is very likely, that's perfect. You have all the answers inside yourself and this will help you pull them out so you can hear them. In my Power Workshops, one person or another would argue fiercely with me about some concept and, in my effort to bring forth my best response, I would hear myself saying something for the first time, something new that increased my own understanding.

The person who takes the other side of this discussion is arguing for his or her limitations. If this person argues well enough and long enough, he or she will get to own those limitations. By taking the position in your discussion that all things *are* possible, you have aligned yourself with that Universal truth that all things are possible for those who know that all things are possible.

As you progress through this program, you will become ever more capable of setting forth reasons and arguments for your position. After a while, you will discard those reasons because you'll be a living demonstration of the truth of your beliefs. Actually, you are now a living demonstration of your beliefs. So stretch your mind to accept entirely that you are capable of accomplishing your goals and desires.

EXERCISE NUMBER TWO

Taking the First Step

Sit quietly for ten minutes in a place where you will be free from interruption. Ask yourself: "Do I have a belief left anywhere in my mind that there is something I will fail at, even if I totally set myself to accomplish it?" If you think of something, carefully remove the limitations from your thinking. Expand your belief system to include being fully capable of accomplishing whatever you want.

The way to do that is to think of what you want and then say to yourself, *"I can do it."* At first you may have to pretend that it's true, but there is a part of you that will hear you say, *"I can do it,"* and will respond accordingly.

When you want to accomplish a goal, the best way to start is always to take the first step toward it, believing that you will achieve your goal. What one step can you take toward fulfilling one of your goals that you have been putting off because you haven't believed you could succeed? Take that step, knowing that it is taking you closer to your heart's desire.

EXERCISE NUMBER THREE

Mentally Complete Events of the Past

Sit quietly for a half hour and remember, beginning with your childhood, the times when you failed at something—failed to start, failed to finish, failed to do. As you remember each event, mentally complete the task or event *in your mind*.

You may use any method you choose, including imaginary superpowers. See the task completed. See yourself looking at the completed project, being congratulated by others for having done a wonderful job. Feel the glow of excellence and completion. Treat yourself to those good feelings.

After you have satisfactorily completed in your imagination whatever it was you failed to do in the past, smile at this past event and go on to the next item. This healing of your past is a mental benefit of the best and most powerful kind. Remember that your subconscious mind does not know the difference between a real event and an imagined event. You are retraining your mind to believe that you are a perfect person, accomplishing all your goals. If you happen to think of one of those "failures" at any time later, smile at it, remind yourself that it is completed, and move on. You're making "Who You Think You Are" whole.

EXERCISE NUMBER FOUR

Learning to Be Happy—Pleasure Exercise #7

Enjoy another half hour of pleasure. Before you choose your pleasure exercise, think about the other six pleasure exercises already completed. Were they fully satisfying? Is there a way you can improve as you treat yourself to a similar experience this time?

In choosing this next exercise, make it extra-special. Fulfill this exercise in the afternoon between the hours of 1 and 6 p.m. Begin by saying, *"I, [say your name], give myself permission to enjoy a half hour of pleasure."*

After the exercise is completed, write a brief summary on the next page under the heading "Pleasure Exercise #7" along with the date you completed the exercise.

Complete the exercises in this chapter before going on to chapter 9.

Pleasure Exercise #7:

Date completed: ______________________________

9

ALL OF YOU

Character is our destiny.
—Heraclitus

IN THE PHYSICAL WORLD, certain metals can be joined together to form a new metal that's many times stronger than the sum of their separate strengths. It's called alloying. Steel, for example, is an alloy of iron and carbon with some other elements. Brass is an alloy of copper and zinc. To alloy means to join together.

The strength of a metal is evaluated by its tensile strength, the ability of a metal to withstand being pulled apart. Suppose we take metal A, which has a tensile strength of four; metal B, which has a tensile strength of two; and metals C and D, each having a tensile strength of five. When we add their separate tensile strengths together, we get a total of sixteen.

It would be logical to assume that if we melted those metals and joined them together (alloyed them), the strength of the new metal would be the total of their separate strengths added together—in this case, sixteen. But when we combine those metals and test the new product, we find that a magical development has occurred—the new product has a tensile strength of forty! A similar thing takes place when you make epoxy. When you buy a package of liquid epoxy, it contains two small vials of fluid. By themselves, they are watery fluids, but when mixed together a chemical reaction occurs and the mixture becomes as hard as iron.

The same type of magical development happens to you when all of your character attributes are present and functioning at 100 percent capacity. What are the character attributes you possess? Look at the following attributes. Briefly think about the meaning of each one. Ask yourself if you possess that particular attribute in sufficient quantity to be all you can be, saying yes or no aloud as you consider each one so that you can hear the answer.

Courage
Mental strength
Dignity
Honesty
Loyalty
Truthfulness
Responsibility
Trustworthiness
Tolerance
Compassion
Kindness
Consideration
Fairness
Morality
Justice

Have you been using those attributes to your full capacity? If you haven't, know that you have limited yourself to obtaining only a small portion of the terrific win that's possible for you.

Knowing that you are a person who uses less than all your attributes influences "Who You Think You Are." When you know that you are sometimes less than fair, less than honest, less than considerate, less than truthful, less than kind and compassionate, less than moral, less than courageous, less than responsible, less than loyal, less than trustworthy, less than tolerant—in short, less than whole—you have a diminished self-image. You project that self-image *constantly*. It affects everything you say, the way you carry yourself, the way you look at people—all of your actions. By functioning with less than your full self, you have done less, had less, and been less than was possible for you.

Just as combining certain metals creates a strong alloy, each time you strengthen one of your character attributes, you become more capable and more powerful. Whenever you increase your character attributes, your self-image ("Who You Think You Are") improves, and then you are stronger and more invincible than ever before. And just as the armor of the knights of old protected them when they went into battle, so your character attributes are invincible shields, protecting you.

HOW MUCH OF YOURSELF DO YOU PUT IN?

Think about the great personal benefits that accompany a life of strength, wholeness, and invincibility. When you bring 100 percent of yourself into your daily life, you create the finest circumstances possible, which you then get to experience.

There's a popular children's song called "The Hokey Pokey." The singers all join hands and form a circle. Their actions follow the words of the song, which go something like this: "You put your left foot in, you put your left foot out, you put your left foot in, and you shake it all about." Later on, you put in your right foot, your right hand, until finally your whole self is in. Think about that song the next time you consider your relationships with others. How much of yourself do you want to put in? Do you only put your left foot in and then sit there wondering why you are getting less from the relationship than you want? *Whatever you bring to the game of your life sets the limit for how much you can get out of life. To have all that you want, bring all that you have!*

In a poker game, where there is betting, whether for money or matchsticks, you must put up an ante. The ante is the stake you put at risk before you can get cards dealt to you. The limit of the game is the largest single bet that a player is allowed to make at any one time. In poker, the limit usually determines what the ante is—the higher the limit, the higher the ante. In the game of your life, it works the opposite way. The ante, what you bring to the game, determines what the limit is. To have what you want, up your personal ante! Raise it to the maximum. You choose the limits of your game.

THE RELATIVE WORLD VERSUS THE ABSOLUTE WORLD

In upping your personal ante, you'll find that you move from the "relative," or "almost," world into the "100 percent," or "absolute," world. Some examples of what it's like to live in the 100 percent, or absolute, world are:

Always arriving for your appointments on time
Always speaking the truth
Starting jobs and completing them
Always keeping your agreements, even with yourself
Completing tasks to your complete satisfaction
Being physically fit
Being completely free of addictions
Completely fulfilling your obligations
Always being reverent
Always being true to what you believe in
Making decisions and acting on them
Always being dependable
Always being fair
Never taking advantage of anyone
Always being courageous
Always being completely trustworthy
Always doing your share and more

The reward for living in the absolute world is that your power will grow and your attainments will be like the harvest after a perfect summer. On the other hand, some examples of living in the relative world are:

Almost being in shape
Almost being on time
Almost being finished
Almost making it
Almost being truthful

Almost being a good friend
Almost being a good partner
Almost being a good mate—*almost, almost, almost*

In that almost-made-it kind of existence, we have second-rate relationships, second-rate accomplishments, and pure, bright human beings acting the part of second-rate people.

I know you've made changes—major changes. But you *can* make even more. You *can* have what you want. You do it by upping your ante. Bring to the game *all* of your honor, *all* of your capability, *all* of your effort, *all* of your courage, *all* of your strength! *Now* is the only chance you have. This time called now is all you ever have. It is all that exists. It is all there is. *The rest is an illusion.* If you don't believe that, try doing something in a time other than now.

This is your moment. *This* is your chance to achieve greatness. *This* is your chance to take off the limits, to participate fully *with all you have*.

What does life have to do with bits and pieces, halves and partials? Why muddy it, halve it, quarter it? Why leave part of yourself at home when you go out to play in the game of your life? Why play with others who have done the same?

Every action produces a result, and the result is in exact accord with the action. That's a Universal law. So if you live your life at less than 100 percent of your potential, you severely limit what you can get from life. *You* put a limit on it. Up your personal ante! Raise it to the maximum. The rewards are colossal, the players are terrific, the game is exciting, and *you* are the winner!

BRINGING MORE OF YOURSELF TO THE GAME OF LIFE

As you bring more and more of yourself to the game of your life, it's helpful to understand more about the attributes that make up you. Here are some perspectives that you may not have considered before about several of these attributes.

Courage. Courage and fear go hand in hand. Courage is what you bring forth to do the things you fear to do. For courage to be necessary, fear *must* be present. Without fear, courage is unnecessary. Fear is a natural stimulus that generates quick activity. It causes adrenalin to be released into your system for a quick, powerful response. In the middle of a street, a car horn startles you and you quickly jump back to avoid being hit. Fear, in that case, is your protector. However, fear, like everything else, can have its negative side. Many fears are born in your imagination and have no basis in real life.

Put this book down for a moment and carefully consider your concept of fear. Do that now before you read on. What do you think about fear?

When you think about fear, you may think in terms of "feeling afraid." If you've focused only on the feeling, which is the immediate effect of fear, then look further because fear is more than that. "Feeling afraid" only means that fear is present, but beyond that immediate feeling of fear is *your expectation of a bad result*. If you were completely certain that the situation would turn out perfectly—in fact, to your greatest benefit—fear would be absent; you would proceed with confidence. On the other hand, if you believe that a situation will have a bad outcome, your belief will produce fear. If you allow the fear to run through you without awakening your courage in response to it, then your fear will block your ability to act.

Where does the fear come from? Is fear present within the situation itself? Of course not. Fear is *purely* a product of your imagination. Without you using your imagination, fear cannot exist. Fear is generated within you only because you imagine the situation turning out badly. Do you let fear block you? Or do you call upon your courage, which then empowers you? Fear can be a crippling emotion, but *only if you fail to respond with courage*. With courage, you can turn the situation into "just another workout situation."

The next time you feel fear and there is time to think about the situation, say the following things to yourself:

1. *This is a workout situation.*
2. *This comes from the circumstances in my own life.*
3. *This is aimed at one of my weak areas.*
4. *The fear that I feel is aimed at my weak area so I can strengthen it.*
5. *There is some information in this situation that I need, and I will get it by going through this.*
6. *Even though I'm afraid, I have enough courage to act.*
7. *I'll feel good about myself for having acted courageously.*

Once you have said those seven statements, imagine a beneficial outcome rather than the one that is causing your fear. Then, *take action to handle the situation*.

Mental Strength (Willpower and Determination). Having mental strength means that you will finish what you begin, that you will persevere to the end even in the face of great adversity. In every situation, even difficult ones, your strength will carry you through to the end. As long as your effort continues, you have not been defeated and, in the end, you will be successful. It is only when you quit that you have failed. Remember what you read earlier: When you have done as much as you absolutely can, when you have given your all, the Universe will step in and give you what you need to get you to the next step.

Dignity. As your awareness and capability grow, so grows your self-respect. Self-respect can become a pitfall if it turns into overbearing swaggering. *Dignity is self-respect at perfect pitch.* It's an internal trait that expresses "Who You Are." You walk into a room confidently, you meet the glance of others directly, and in conversation your words are chosen carefully. Dignity and profanity are a poor mix; the one cancels out the other. Having dignity means that you will refrain from doing certain things—things that would be out of character for a person of noble ideals. As you achieve dignity, everyone you meet will sense "Who You Are" and treat you accordingly. It's the Universal law of cause and effect, and it can be no other way.

Honesty. Honesty, in the sense I'm using it, is more than telling the truth. Honesty is also not taking that which does not belong to you, giving a proper remuneration for value received, dealing squarely with others, not taking advantage of anyone, being fair, keeping your word, and fulfilling your obligations. There is probably no more effective way to improve on what you think of yourself than by being an honest person. It is a trait highly valued by all clear-thinking people.

Loyalty. Loyalty is being faithful to a person or cause. When you have a friend, you owe it to that person and to yourself to be a supporter of that person in every way. If you are in a relationship, you owe it to the person with whom you are in the relationship to be a supporter of that person. Giving aid to someone you have a relationship with makes you feel good about yourself. That's a benefit all by itself.

Truthfulness. Truthfulness is truth-fullness. That means all the truth, all the time. The only reason you ever lied was because you were afraid. Fear again! You knew what the truth was, but you felt that if you told it, you would experience a bad outcome. You wanted to avoid that outcome, so, in your mind, you reshaped what actually happened or was going to happen, and you told it in a way that tricked your listener into believing your new version.

Does distorting the truth change the reality of what is? What happened still happened. The real truth, which lives within you, remains the same. Your saying it differently only makes it more difficult to work with. It's a seed you plant in yourself that you then have to carry around while it grows. If you are in a situation where you feel you must lie, use the same steps I suggested you use when confronted with a fearful situation (page 182), affirming those seven statements and seeing a beneficial outcome from being truthful. Taking these steps will bring about the same freedom-producing results because all lying is based upon fear.

Telling the truth will bring you directness of mind, meaning your mind will not be cluttered with the effort of creating and maintaining a lie. The waste of energy and time you use in planning, executing, and maintaining a lie will be eliminated from your life, giving you back your undivided, whole self. Your future will be free from waste and division.

You'll be complete in your energy and attention. You will enjoy straight thinking and straight talking, which will bring you straight to your goals.

Responsibility. Being responsible means that you can be given a task and you can be relied upon to do it and do it well. It also means that you will refrain from acts that are foolhardy. A responsible person does not needlessly put himself or herself at risk or put others needlessly at risk. Being responsible means people can trust you and not have their trust betrayed.

Trustworthiness. Trustworthiness means you can be relied upon, that you can be trusted to speak the truth, and that you can be trusted to do what you say you will do. When you are trustworthy, you are the kind of person others want as a friend. Sometimes having a good friend is the most important asset one can have.

Tolerance. Being tolerant of others goes beyond forgiveness. It means forgiving others' intentional offenses and violations as well as overlooking their mistakes, shortcomings, and faults. Forgiveness, of course, implies that someone did something that was truly bad for you. But by now you should know that's not possible, even if the person's intention was to hurt you.

Kindness. Kindness means treating others with compassion, tenderness, good-heartedness, gentleness, and tolerance. When you are kind to others, you are doing them a favor or overlooking a fault or going out of your way to do something nice for them.

Consideration. When you are considerate of another, you will carefully think about the outcome of your actions with regard to that person. You will take into account how he or she will be affected by your action, and then you will act in such a manner as to not hurt that person by your action.

Fairness. Being fair means that you will not take advantage of others in your dealings with them. Fairness, as well as all the other characteristics listed here, is an excellent characteristic for a leader to have. When you are fair, you do not take more than your share. When acting on behalf of a group, you look out for the welfare of others along with your own, even if the group is composed of just you and one other person. A person who is fair is a good choice when it comes to finding someone who will care for others.

Morality. Having morality means you make the right decision between right and wrong. Being a moral person means you act with virtue. With regard to sexual matters, you act rightly and not in an immoral manner. When you have morality as a characteristic, you tend toward good conduct in all areas of your life.

EXERCISE NUMBER ONE

Seeing Yourself with the Attributes of an Invincible, Powerful, Whole Person

Decide for yourself the degree to which you aspire to be a person of power, virtue, integrity, and invincibility. See yourself in your mind's eye as that person. When you take the alpha-level journey, know that your perfect image already has all those attributes in the maximum amount possible. When you merge with your perfect image, you clothe yourself with all those attributes.

Study the definitions of each of the characteristics described in this chapter until you feel you know, fully, what each one means and the degree to which you possess each one.

Momentarily imagine yourself having each attribute and see how it feels. This imagining process is of great importance, so spend some time doing it well. When you have alloyed those powerful character attributes within yourself, you will have attained the stature of a person who is immune to harm. The ancient Chinese sages, when referring to such a person, said: "Even the fiercest attack harmlessly glances off of him or her."

Complete this first exercise before going on to the next exercise.

EXERCISE NUMBER TWO

Up the Ante

Find a quiet, comfortable place to sit. On the next page under the heading "Ways I Will Up My Personal Ante," begin your list of ways you will bring all of yourself to the game of life, such as being more truthful, being more considerate, working more diligently to complete your goals, thinking better of yourself, and, most important, vowing to follow the philosophy you are learning in this book.

Be specific when you write the ways you will up your ante. If you write that you will bring more of yourself to a personal relationship, write *how* you will do that. If you resolve to do a job better, say *how* you are going to do it better—and then make certain you follow through. At the end of your list, sign your name. Be most particular in how you are going to follow your new philosophy, as it is the major factor, the key, to being who you want and having what you want.

Read your list every day for the next month. Mark your calendar now. It will help if you read it aloud, even if you just whisper it. Make copies of your list to tape to your mirrors (car, bathroom, bedroom, etc.), to put by your favorite chair, and to carry with you in your purse, wallet, day planner, or briefcase.

Your will is the constant force that will bring the items on your list into being. Make it happen! Fulfilling this exercise well is a way of strengthening yourself so you can live as a powerful, shining force. By your willpower alone, you can raise your consciousness to the level where the things that you want come to life and come to you. All you need to do is up your personal ante. Add new items to your list when you think of them.

Ways I Will Up My Personal Ante:

Signature:________________________________ **Date:**__________

EXERCISE NUMBER THREE

Tell the Truth

Think of a misrepresentation you have made to someone—a lie you've told, even if it was an exaggeration or an omission of facts. (Don't delude yourself that you have not lied to someone; you have.)

Before you read the next chapter, find the person or people and tell them the truth. This is hard! But remember, you are doing this for yourself. Also remember that you created this as a workout situation in the first place. This course of action is designed to make you into the kind of person you need to be in order to have what you want. Do it—and do it well.

EXERCISE NUMBER FOUR

Learning to Be Happy—Pleasure Exercise #8:

Enjoy another half hour of pleasure. Begin by saying, *"I, [say your name], give myself permission to enjoy a half hour of pleasure."* Choose an activity that is different from the other pleasure exercises you chose. Prepare for it. Do what you can to make it extra nice. Make it a celebration of being here on Earth.

After the exercise is completed, write a brief summary on the next page under the heading "Pleasure Exercise #8" along with the date you completed your pleasure exercise.

Complete the exercises in this chapter before going on to chapter 10.

Pleasure Exercise #8:

Date completed: ______________________________

10

COMMITMENT

Once the what *is decided, the* how *always follows. We must not make the* how *an excuse for not facing and accepting the* what.
—*Pearl S. Buck*

THERE IS A BEAUTIFUL LINE from one of the works of the Indian poet and philosopher Rabindranath Tagore that goes like this: "I have spent my days stringing and unstringing my instrument while the song I came to sing remains unsung." Those words speak of this moment in your life when it's time to express yourself as the great human being you are and to begin to sing the song you came to sing. You are the song. You came to earth to sing your song. It's time for you to do that now. For you to sing your song, commitment is essential. You must learn what commitment means and use it as one of the most important tools in your arsenal.

The word *commitment*, as it is generally used, is interchangeable with the word *promise*, but promises are sometimes broken. In this program, the word *commitment* has a different meaning, a special meaning. It means *"that which is fulfilled."* Making a commitment and fulfilling it *are one and the same* because when you make a commitment and fully understand what it means, the power to fulfill your commitment arises at the same time.

So from this time forward, when you make a commitment, what you are committed to is the same as done. If for any reason you fail in your commitment, then what you thought was a commitment was only a promise or a plan that, in the end, you failed to accomplish. It is essential that you understand the difference between a commitment and a promise or a plan.

To move forward in this program and on your path, when you make a commitment, fulfill it under *all* circumstances, letting your total commitment take you to your goal. Of course, that means you must be careful about what you commit to, because once you have committed yourself, you are duty-bound to stay with your commitment until you have fulfilled it.

There is only one constant in your life: You. Friends pass away, parents or guardians pass away, partners and associates pass away, situations change. Only you remain as a constant in every plan you make. If you cannot rely upon yourself *totally* to see your plans through to successful ends, every plan you make will be flawed. Every plan will have the possibility of failure.

Once you are able to make a commitment in the way I am using that word here, you will endow your every project with success. You will be able to depend on yourself. Can you see the power of that? That means you will no longer be at the mercy of others to see your projects through to a successful conclusion. Even if everyone around you falters, you will see your plans through to a successful end.

SEEING IT THROUGH

The Power Workshops that I held were four weeks long, five nights a week, for one hour each night. One workshop, therefore, consisted of twenty meetings over the course of twenty-six days. As I wrote earlier, at the close of the first night's meeting, everyone who wanted to continue was required to make a commitment to be present at the remaining nineteen meetings and to be there on time. If a participant failed to appear on time or missed a meeting for *any reason whatsoever*, he or she had to drop out of the course and wait for a new course to begin.

Some participants objected to this policy. They said it overlooked valid reasons for being absent or late. They failed to see that it was those same "valid reasons" that had given them the right to fail in other situations, the right to have less than they wanted and the right to be powerless throughout their lives.

In the workshops, *all* reasons for failing met the same fate. Only those who overcame all obstacles and came to every meeting on time were at the final meeting. They, too, had encountered problems and difficulties that could have prevented them from fulfilling their commitment, but they overcame every obstacle. They, too, could have thought of "valid reasons" for coming late or missing a meeting, but they chose to see it through, overcoming everything that came along. They had decided they had had enough of the way things were for them, and so they put forth the necessary effort to be at every meeting, on time. They were committed.

Two weeks into one workshop, a man who had made incredible progress in his first two weeks didn't come to a

Friday workshop. The following Monday he came to the door on crutches. He had broken his foot two hours before the Friday workshop. I refused him admittance. He was outraged. He told me he desperately needed the workshop and that he had made more progress in his life in the past two weeks than he had ever made in his life. He said a broken foot was a valid reason for missing the workshop.

I told him that all his life he had found valid reasons for failing and that this was just another one of those reasons. He yelled at me, "But my foot was broken!" I told him that he could have come to the workshop with a broken foot. He could have just as well had his foot put into a cast after the workshop as before it. I pointed out to him that the amount of power he would have gained from coming to the workshop with a broken foot would have been enough to accomplish any goal he ever chose from that moment forward. Instead, he did what he usually did; he chose not to honor his commitment. He chose failure.

This is a black-and-white issue. There are no halfway measures here. Get used to that idea. You must be able to rely on yourself *completely*. No excuses. You either do or you don't. All the excuses that exist are the same; they are reasons for failing to fulfill your commitment. No one of them is better than another, and all lead to failure. That's not for you. Here's something that will be a huge bonus for you in making commitments. W. H. Murray, the Scottish mountaineer, wrote these timeless and empowering words about commitment:

> Until one is committed, there is hesitancy, the chance to draw back, always ineffectiveness. Concerning all acts of initiative (and creation), there is one elemen-

> tary truth the ignorance of which kills countless ideas and splendid plans: that the moment one definitely commits oneself, *then providence moves too* [emphasis added]. A whole stream of events issues from the decision, raising in one's favor all manner of unforeseen incidents, meetings and material assistance, which no man could have dreamt would have come his way. I learned a deep respect for one of Goethe's couplets: Whatever you can do or dream you can, begin it. Boldness has genius, power and magic in it!

OVERCOMING RESISTANCE WITH COMMITMENT

Do you know any good reason for failing to live the life you want? When you're committed to living the life of the aware and the capable, your need for "excuses" and "reasons for failing" disappears. Success is the only road open to you.

Sally, a workshop participant in her early forties, wanted very much to fulfill her commitment to be at all the workshop meetings, but she had a problem. Several months before the workshop began, Sally had made a plan to go skiing with her family and friends. The date they had set turned out to be during the third week of the workshop. In the second week of the workshop, Sally told us that she wanted to finish the workshop but that she had always been a weak person and her husband was very pushy. Sally said he was going to insist that she go as planned, and she was afraid she would give in.

I asked Sally if she had made a commitment to go on the trip with her family. She said she hadn't, but it was generally assumed by her family that she would go. I reminded her that she had made a commitment to attend all the workshop meetings and that all she needed was the absolute intention to fulfill her commitment to be present at all the remaining meetings of the workshop. I also told her that the capability as well as the solution was *within her*.

As the appointed day of departure neared, Sally became more and more nervous. She wanted to believe what I was telling her, yet she was still afraid she would give in to the pressure. She said her family was arguing with her every day about going. She, on the other hand, was remaining adamant that she was going to fulfill her commitment to attend all the workshop meetings.

At the workshop, the night before her family was leaving for the trip, we talked about it for the last time. All the other people attending the workshop also gave her encouragement not to give in. I again told her that everything would turn out perfectly if she would only stick to her decision to fulfill her commitment. I explained that this was an opportunity for her to take a giant step—a chance to break the control of those who were always making her decisions for her against her will. Those circumstances, emerging out of the framework of her own life, had brought about "the perfect next step" whereby she could achieve the strength she needed. All she had to do was call on her courage, face her situation, and come to the next workshop meeting.

The following night, Sally was absent. When she returned from her skiing trip, she telephoned and said she had waited for the solution to turn up "right until the last second," and then, because she failed to see any way out, she went on the trip.

Sally had waited for the solution to occur as if the solution had a mind of its own and was going to happen by itself. Who packed Sally's bags? Who walked out of Sally's house to the car? Who went on the trip? Sally's solution was there all the time. She simply could have told her family that although she had made a plan to go skiing, she had since that time made a commitment to complete the workshop, a commitment that was more important to her than the skiing trip. She could have told them that during her lifetime she had been a weak person and this was a wonderful opportunity for her to become strong, and if they would support her decision, they would all benefit from it. She could have also explained that the skiing trip would be over when her family returned home, but the benefits of her completing the workshop would go on and on.

Her family, sensing her lack of true commitment, simply did what they had always done—they bent her to their will. If she had been truly committed to completing the workshop, her family would have felt that absolute force and Sally would have had her way. She would have overcome their resistance, gaining her much-needed freedom in the process.

RELYING FULLY ON YOURSELF

The way to perfect your ability to make true commitments is clear: *Choose and act on a commitment.* Once you've made a commitment, understanding all that it means, you will be seen as a powerful person, and others will respect you and deal with you as such. Once you've made a commitment, others will fail to sway you; they will fail in all attempts to divert you from your course of action. By committing yourself, in the true sense of the word, *you have already succeeded.*

At the moment of true commitment, you are a source of great power. How much? As much as is needed to fulfill your commitment. If you have any doubts or reservations, if you have failed to be completely at one with your commitment, you will always be hesitant. You will always have less than 100 percent of your effort directed at a precise outcome. You will always be less than completely effective. You will always entertain the possibility in your mind that you can draw back. That possibility will prevent you from tapping into your own strength fully. *When it comes to commitment, there is only one possible outcome.*

Remember, this is a black-and-white issue; all the gray areas are gone. There are few who speak of commitment with the meaning that you now understand. Nearly everyone accepts indecision, excuses, weakness, and reasons for failing. Nearly everyone allows for the gray areas. For the most part, it's the gray areas that have regularly caused failure in your life. It's the gray areas that prevent you from living in the world of the absolute and keep you living in the relative world of "almost" and "might have been." In that world, there are acceptable reasons for failing. In the world of commitment, failure is absent. To exist there, it is essential that you be able to rely upon yourself *fully*.

When you fail to go forth resolutely, you are ill-equipped to deal with situations adequately. Pay attention to the words *resolutely* and *adequately*. They mean that if you want to have enough of whatever it takes to reach every goal, you have to commit yourself to overcoming *all* obstacles. As the opening quotation of this chapter from Pearl S. Buck advises, also be sure not to let your aha moment, your initial inspiration, be spoiled by wondering how you are going to bring it off. When you have complete determination, you go forth with the correct attitude, which carries you through to your goal. *Everyone stands aside to let a determined person go by.*

After you have come to the point of knowing that you can *totally* rely on yourself, you will radiate such power and great self-confidence that others will trust you and ask you to be part of their plans. You will be much sought after. People will know they can depend on you. They will naturally trust your judgment and your capability. Promotions and opportunities of all kinds will be offered to you. Your image will radiate control and doing-ness. In your mind, your range of achievable goals will expand greatly. This will step up the whole process of changing "Who You Think You Are" into a new image of power and capability.

Imagine an archer about to shoot an arrow. The archer stands with the bowstring fully drawn back, the arrow pointed directly at its goal. Now the archer looses the string and, in that moment of release, the arrow speeds forward, totally committed to reaching its goal. Imagine yourself as that arrow, committed to absolutely reaching your goal—acknowledging that you will overcome all obstacles, that you will surmount all problems, that you will, under every condition imaginable and beyond imagination, attain your goal.

What that means is that you will call upon *every ounce of power, strength, and determination* that you possess in order to fulfill what you have irrevocably committed yourself to. When you set yourself up with that attitude—to absolutely fulfill your projects, goals, and desires—obstacles and difficulties will *dissolve in the face of your total determination*. You can then let your imagination roam through the world of possibilities, choosing that which you want, knowing that you are a person who can and will fulfill your plans and achieve your goals.

The idea of failure should be eliminated from your thinking. Remember that Thomas Edison conducted thousands of experiments in his quest to invent what we now know as the lightbulb. "The electric light has caused me the greatest amount of study and has required the most elaborate experiments," he later wrote. "I was never myself discouraged, or inclined to be hopeless of success. I cannot say the same for all my associates." When a reporter asked Edison how it felt to fail two thousand times before successfully inventing the lightbulb, Edison is said to have responded: "I never failed once. It just happened to be a two-thousand-step process."

Failure only occurs when you quit. Until then, you are always in the process of fulfilling your commitment. Seeming failures and setbacks are just ways the Universe increases your strength, your determination, and your will to win.

THE EFFORT IS WORTH IT

As I was working on this section of the book, I received the following letter from a woman who had been working with an earlier version of this book. Her letter shows that change is possible when we commit to the work that is needed to bring about real change. The changes you desire are just as possible for you.

Hello Chris:

March 1st marked a milestone: after nine months of work, I finished your book, including the exercises at the end of each chapter. I've shared the information in this book with many people since I found it and have begun to buy copies to give to others. It requires discipline and hard work, but is well worth the time and effort.

In the past nine months, I have closed a failing business, put my condo up for sale, found a stunningly perfect job, and gotten engaged. When the condo sells, my 11-year-old son and I will move in with my fiancé. You taught me about commitment, the existence of my perfect self and how to visualize her, and that everything that has come before in my life has been perfect. My view needed adjustment.

I was ready to do your work. From beating my alcoholism at 22 and then the drug addiction that followed in my early 30s, to being a student of more enlightened writers like yourself for over a decade, there remained areas in my life that would improve and then get messy again. One author talks about climbing the stairs in Love's House and how we sometimes have to go back down to lower levels because we didn't take care of the mess before we tried to go upstairs. Well, sometimes one has to learn to clean, but has no idea what tools to use. You gave me the additional tools I needed. You also helped me see that my perfectionism and Gifted-ness are and always have been a gift. How I view and use them gives them their power.

Thank you. I wish you all good things in your journey.

EXERCISE NUMBER ONE

Committing to a Major Goal and Taking the First Step

Think of something you want to do in your life, something that will be a major accomplishment for you. It might be straightening out or ending a long-term relationship. It might be changing jobs or leaving your home. Perhaps it is making a decision to marry or begin a partnership, overcoming an unhealthy habit or addiction that has burdened you for a long time, or deciding to finally overcome a long illness. Maybe it's ending financial or emotional dependence on someone, learning a martial art, or getting in top physical condition. It might be taking a long trip, starting a retirement program, or fulfilling another plan you have been waiting to put into action for many years.

Whatever it is, *commit to doing it now*. Then take the first step, which is to turn to the page at the end of this exercise headed "My Commitment" and write down your commitment. Be clear and precise about what it is.

Next, underneath that, write the first steps that you will take to fulfill your commitment. If you can think only of the first step at this time, that is sufficient. When your goal is still far off, you may only be able to see the first step to reaching it. But as you approach the goal, the path will become clearer because what was at first far away is now near.

As you think of additional steps that will lead to your goal, add them to your list. As you accomplish steps on the way to your goal, draw a light line through them and write down the date you completed them. It is sometimes very helpful to work backwards. Think of the last step to achieving your goal, then the one before that, and so on, until you get back to the present.

Review your list every morning to see what you can do that day to move toward your goal, even though it might be only a small step. Review the list every night to see what you have accomplished that day and to plan for the next day. Each time you are able to cross off a completed step, you will feel a comforting sense of satisfaction—and you will be one step closer to accomplishing your goal.

If you are not sure what steps to take to reach your goal, imagine you are going on a journey. First you need to decide where you are going and what you want to do when you arrive. Then you need to determine what you need to do before you go. You'll also need to decide what you want to take with you.

When you make a commitment to accomplish a major goal, go through those same steps. Decide on your goal, what you need to do to accomplish it, and what you need in hand to be successful. Remember the ancient saying: "A journey of a thousand miles begins with a single step." And *the first step is always directly in front of you.*

As soon as you have chosen your major goal, acknowledge in your mind that you have already attained it. Act as if you have attained it. The Universe is required to respond to you at every moment, and therefore it will respond by acknowledging your attainment.

Along the path to your goal, you will gain strength, wisdom, power, and happiness. In the end, you will discover that the path that led to your goal, rather than reaching the goal itself, was the most important part of your journey. It is along that path that your life will unfold.

I wish you an exciting, fulfilling journey. When you have committed yourself to fulfilling the major goal you chose, you will soon begin feeling the excitement that comes with your knowledge that you will attain it.

Once you have decided on your major goal, made your written commitment to reach it, and listed the first steps you need to take in order to reach it, move on to the next exercise.

My Commitment:

Signature:_______________________________ **Date:**__________

EXERCISE NUMBER TWO

Learning to Be Happy—Pleasure Exercise #9

Enjoy another half hour of pleasure. Begin by saying, *"I, [say your name], give myself permission to enjoy a half hour of pleasure."* Fulfill this exercise in the morning, sometime between the hours of 6 a.m. and 10 a.m., on any day you choose. If it is convenient, fulfill the exercise outdoors.

After the exercise is completed, write a brief summary on the next page under the heading "Pleasure Exercise #9." Many years from now, you will treasure your summaries.

Complete the exercises in this chapter before going on to chapter 11.

Pleasure Exercise #9:

Date completed: ______________________________

11

SAYING IT POSITIVE

Spartans, stoics, heroes, saints and gods use a short and positive speech. They are never off their centres.
—Ralph Waldo Emerson

MANY OF THE SENTENCES WE SAY are spoken in negative terms, such as "I don't think I'll go" or "I don't think I want any of that." But what does "don't think" mean? How do you go about "don't thinking"? You can say that it's just "a manner of speaking," but the manner matters—a lot. When you think and speak negatively, you produce negative results. The opposite is also true.

Your manner of speaking *is* you. Everything that you say and everything that you do comes from your state of being at the moment of saying or doing. Everything that flows from you comes from who and what you are. If you are angry, you speak from your angry center. Your words are tinged with anger and their meaning conveys anger.

In reality, negative statements have very little power. The small amount of power they do have is present only because the listener's mind turns the statement around to its positive form first. For example, when you say to someone, "Don't go outside," the listener's mind automatically turns that into its positive form in order to be able to understand it: "Stay inside." If you say, "Don't think about a purple poodle," what happens? Your mind automatically sees that image.

To move away from negativity and become a more powerful person, put substance into your words. Instead of saying, "I am not going to go," say what you are going to do, such as "I am going to stay at home." People need to have something substantial to react to. If you speak negatively, you can expect that you will often be ignored and misunderstood, and you will have only a small amount of influence.

Here's an example. Suppose we were walking down a steep trail with a sharp drop on one side and I wanted to tell you, "Watch where you're going." Suppose I said it in its negative form, "Don't watch where you're not going." You would have to puzzle it out and finally come to the conclusion that if you are *not* to watch where you're *not* going, then you *are* to watch where you *are* going. That's an extreme example, but negatives are like that.

For your words to have power, they must have direction and force—"I am going to climb the mountain," "I am going to get the job," "I will win the prize." You could also say to someone, "Please go outside and play rather than standing in front of me bouncing that ball." That's a better choice of words than something vague like "Don't do that!" Give direction—say what will be, and it will be! This takes practice and your progress may be gradual, but you will notice the difference as you begin to speak positively.

GIVE UP TRYING

Tried is another word for *failed*. Used in the past tense, it *always* means that we have failed. If you say, "I tried to climb the mountain," you mean, "I attempted to climb the mountain, but I failed." And then you would give the reason why you failed to do so, such as "I tried to climb the mountain but it was too steep" or ". . . but it started to snow." If you had attempted the climb and accomplished it, you wouldn't say, "I tried to climb the mountain." Instead, you would say, "I climbed the mountain."

Listen to yourself and see how often you say, "I'll try." Realize that *try* is a word we use to prepare for failure. It's a way of excusing yourself from doing the hard work of accomplishing whatever it was you set out to do. It gives you something to fall back on in case of failure—"I didn't say I *would* do it; I said I'd *try* to do it." Saying "I'll try" makes it a little easier to fail.

When you were a child, perhaps you were brave enough to say, "I am going to do this!" Perhaps after having said that, you made your brave attempt and failed. Perhaps someone made fun of you because of it or you were made to pay some other price. As a result, you may have felt that you needed to be more careful in how you spoke. So you learned to say, "Well, I'm going to give it my best try, but it's really tough," and that provided an excuse to fall back on.

It's understandable where this habit came from, but it does prepare the way for failure. You came to see failure in the world around you as an acceptable part of being human. The real problem with this stems from your knowing that every time you have used the word *tried*, in the past tense, you have failed at something. After a while, *tried* became synonymous with failure in your mind. Therefore, when you use the word *try*, as in "I will try to do this or that," the subconscious part of you associates it with failure. It's time to drop that belief.

POSITIVE SPEECH AND POSITIVE INTENTIONS

Trying to do something is an admirable act; accomplishing it takes real courage. It takes a lot of courage to say, "I will do it!" meaning exactly that. It's part of the path to having what you want. It's perfectly all right to say, "I will do it." If you make your first attempt to do something and have a *seeming* failure, as long as you haven't given up in your attempt, you are in the process of fulfilling your intention to do whatever it was you set out to do; you are still on your way to achievement. The only time you fail is when you stop in your efforts to accomplish your goal with the intention of remaining stopped and you say, "Well, I tried." Those words signal your defeat.

Failure is *partly* the result of speaking in negative terms. It is *entirely* the result of thinking in negative terms. There are no rewards for speaking in negative terms. On the other hand, the rewards for speaking in positive terms are sensational. The whole Universe responds to you with direct, positive energy. How else could it respond? The Universe is set up to react in a manner that corresponds to your own. Your speech, therefore, gives substance to your success by declaring in positive terms what your intentions are.

By speaking positively, you will find your thoughts clarified, your speech direct, and the response of others rewarding. You will have an ever-increasing command over how life will be for you. The positive power of your words and intentions will shape the future, revealing the perfect place in which you are meant to naturally exist.

EXERCISE NUMBER ONE

Eliminating Negatives from Your Speech

For the rest of today and all of tomorrow, listen to how you say what you want, and as often as you can, speak in positive terms. Leave out all negative words or phrases, especially those that include the word *not—cannot, do not,* or *will not*. You will see to what extent you have learned to speak negatively by how hard it is to speak positively.

At first, this task can be extremely frustrating. It can take months or even years of practice before you begin to habitually speak positively. Keep at it, though, as the rewards will be substantial. If you are involved in an important conversation and it becomes too frustrating to your conversation to continue speaking only in positive terms, stop this exercise until your conversation is over and then pick it up again.

Today you can begin to throw off more of the self-defeating beliefs that negativity and failure have any place in your speech or in your world. Do whatever you need to do to keep yourself alert to what you are saying. You can write yourself reminder notes and place them in key places or carry a small stone or some other object with you that will remind you to speak positively each time you speak. If you are in a conversation of lesser importance with others for more than a few minutes, tell them about this exercise so they will be patient with you while you find positive expressions for your thoughts.

When this task begins to look impossible, and it will seem that way, or when it becomes so frustrating that you would like to give up, remind yourself of the reasons you have taken on this enormous task.

To have come this far in the program is to be well along the path to achieving your goals and becoming the person you want to be.

Habit will cause you to say things in their negative form. Simply correct yourself and keep going. Continue your efforts to speak positively for all of today and all of tomorrow and consider this exercise complete.

EXERCISE NUMBER TWO

Learning to Be Happy—Pleasure Exercise #10

Enjoy another half hour of pleasure. Begin by saying, *"I, [say your name], give myself permission to enjoy a half hour of pleasure."* Fulfill this exercise in the evening between the hours of 6 p.m. and 11 p.m. on any day you choose.

After the exercise is completed, write a brief summary on the next page under the heading "Pleasure Exercise #10."

Complete the exercises in this chapter before going on to chapter 12.

Pleasure Exercise #10:

Date completed: ______________________________

12

GIVING UP STRESS

The mind is its own place, and in itself
Can make a Heaven of Hell, a Hell of Heaven.
—John Milton

WHEN SOMETHING IMPORTANT TO YOU begins to seemingly go wrong, when your day and its plans seem to be falling apart, you may find yourself tempted to question the perfection of your world. When several such moments occur close together, you may begin to feel some serious tension. It's worse when there is a time frame involved, such as having to accomplish a task by a certain time or you will have irrevocably failed, as in catching a plane. By allowing this tension or stress to continue, *you ensure its growing presence in your life*. Over a period of time, stress can cause many physical ailments.

The title of this chapter, "Giving Up Stress," largely gives you the solution to this problem. You may have thought that the exterior situations and events that have occurred in your life created stress. As an aware person, you now know that it is *you* who decides how you want to feel about the situations in your life. If your stress level remains forever at the mercy of the events that occur around you, your stress level will go up and down like a cork on the ocean as your view of the situations and events appears to have good or bad significance for you. Living a stress-free life is a result of being knowledgeable, being in control, and getting practice—lots of practice.

One evening, about ten days into one of my Power Workshops, I arrived at the place where we were meeting for the workshop to see a cluster of people standing around a new car talking excitedly. Later that evening, I congratulated the owner, Doris, on her new acquisition. I told her I had seen the car and its group of admirers outside. She surprised me by explaining that it wasn't her new car that everyone was so excited about but her reaction to the car's smashed fender. It had been smashed that very morning—just one day after she bought the car! When she first entered the garage in her condominium complex that morning and saw the fender smashed, she felt a severe letdown. She had waited so long for her new car! But then Doris suddenly remembered what she had learned at the Power Workshop—that this was somehow a perfect opportunity—and she looked at the smashed fender with new vision.

"Perfect!" she said, not quite believing it. "Perfect, that's just perfect," she kept telling herself.

YOU ARE IN CHARGE OF YOUR REACTIONS

Doris began to act and treat the situation as though it were the best possible event that could have happened to her.

Doris's enthusiasm and excitement came from no longer being at the mercy of the endless stream of seemingly unfortunate incidents that occur in everyday life. Before she had acquired her attitude that all events are perfect, she would have spent the day feeling despondent and let down. Doris said she might have even gone back to bed to let the day pass before more bad things happened to her.

But that day was different. She made that day into a kind of birthday—the first day of a new kind of life. Beginning that day, Doris was in control of how things were going to be for her, and she decided that they were going to be just perfect. She was free from what she called the "tyranny of events," those incidents that come to us all—the lost watch, the stolen wallet, the missed bus or plane, the telephone call that brings seemingly bad news, the depressing events on the TV news.

Take a moment now and imagine what it would mean for you to be free from the bad side effects that result from the seemingly unfortunate mishaps that regularly occur in your life. If you fail to realize that you are in charge of your reactions and that how you react contributes to the creation of the immediate future, you will continue to create many stressful hours for yourself. When a seemingly bad event occurs, see it as though it were a good event—the best possible event. Treating it that way is *the* major step to giving up stress.

BE LIKE A MOUNTAIN

In the beginning, you may have to pretend that events are perfect. When you are able to naturally react as though everything were for your benefit, that's when life becomes sweet. As the continuing parade of events passes through your life, be like a mountain—while the storms come and go, the winds blow, the sun shines, and the events occur, the mountain remains solid and calm.

Do you spend time regretting the events of the past, saying to yourself, "If only it could have been different" or "If only I would have done this instead of that" or "I wish that wouldn't have happened?" When you think about the way things should have been or could have been but weren't, you're creating stress for yourself. You're also creating unhappiness for yourself.

I had a friend, Frank, who died years ago. Many times during the thirty-year period we knew each other, he said to me, "I sure wish I had gone to college! That was the biggest mistake I ever made, not going to college." Just after Frank graduated from high school, he had the opportunity to begin college, but instead he went to work as a laborer. For thirty-odd years he regretted his choice. What he liked to say was "If only I had gone to college, things would be different for me now."

Frank paid a heavy price by thinking he had made a mistake in choosing not to go to college. He continued to pay the same price over and over during all those thirty years. Whenever there was bad weather and he had to go to work, he would say, "If only I had gone to college, I wouldn't have to be working outside in the rain today," and he would again regret his decision. Frank mentally beat himself up like that for all those years. I never once heard him say, "Gee, this is such a great day today and I get to work outside." Frank saw only the negative side of his situation—and he never decided to go to college. During all the days and years of his lament, it never occurred to him that he could go to college or night school or business school at any moment he chose. *Remember, events are just events; how you react to them determines how they continue to affect you.*

THE ONLY POSSIBILITY

Part of learning how to give up stress is understanding that when an event becomes reality, it was the only possibility. To clarify that, I'll say it another way: Given all that went before—and all that did not go before—what happened was the only possibility.

Here's an exaggerated, imagined example that will help you understand that point. Let's say at the beginning of last spring you decided that you would like to grow tomatoes in your backyard. Here are a few of the things that did happen. You got the idea to plant tomatoes, you went to the store and bought tomato seeds, you came back home, you got out the gardening tools, you went into your backyard, you prepared the soil, you put the seeds in, you covered the seeds with soil, and you watered the soil. In the weeks that passed, the sun shone and you continued to provide water and food for the tomato plants. In time, they matured and produced an abundance of tomatoes.

Here are some of the things that did not happen. You did not get an idea to plant corn instead of tomatoes. You did not buy pumpkin seeds at the store by mistake. You did not go on a long vacation rather than going back home with the tomato seeds. Upon arriving home, you did not get a grinder from the shed and grind the tomato seeds into pulp. You did not plant the seeds in cement rather than soil. You did not leave the seeds uncovered so the birds could eat them. In fact, a bird did not come and eat them. You did not drown the seeds with water.

During the weeks that passed, a garbage truck did not drive over your seeds and smash them into the earth, neither did a plane crash on your tomato plants as they were growing, nor did the bugs come and eat your plants, nor did an earthquake open a crevice under your plants and swallow them into the ground. Those are just some of the many things that did not happen. As you can imagine, the list of things that did not happen is truly endless. So, given all that did happen and all that did not happen, what finally happened was the *only* possibility. I want you to realize that as a complete, absolute truth. What happened was the *only* possibility, given all that did and did not take place beforehand.

Once an event has occurred, your job is to look at it as being *the only event that was possible*. If there were people involved who seemed to have had several choices open to them, realize that whatever choice they made was their *only choice possible*. You may find this difficult to agree with because they had several choices available, perhaps many choices. But this is the main point: When you take into consideration all the factors involved in the situation, what did and did not happen, the choice they made was the only one possible given the circumstances that led up to the situation. The truth is that if the same conditions are present with the same people, they will do the same thing, over and over, as long as the conditions are identical and they have no prior knowledge as to how the event will turn out.

You may find yourself saying to someone, "You could have done that differently" or "You didn't have to say that" or "Why didn't you do this instead of what you did?" Saying those kinds of things only creates stress. When you're arguing with someone about the way something could have been done or should have been done, realize that the person was *only* capable of doing it in the one way he or she did at that moment, given all that went before and all that did not go before.

If you have a hard time agreeing with this concept at first, look at it in terms of your own life. Let's use this book as an example. Your decision to read this book has been a product of all that has gone before in your life. If none of those circumstances or events changed in the slightest, and if you remained exactly the person you were before you decided to read this book, you would, based on whatever made you decide to read this book in the first place, make the same decision, *every single time*. And that would be a result of all that occurred before you made the decision and all that did not occur before you made the decision.

The same is true for all the things you have done in your lifetime. This is of huge importance, so follow it closely. The choices you made in the past and the events that occurred in the past that continue to make you feel bad *were the only choices and events that could have possibly occurred* given all that went before and all that did not go before. If you could go into the past and return to an event that occurred in your life, one that you regret, and if you could relive that event and what led up to it, second by second, knowing *all* the elements that went into creating the event, you would clearly see at the end of your journey that what happened was *the only possibility*.

You would see that if you were the exact same person in the exact same circumstances, you would always make the exact same choice. There is no other possibility.

Looking at everything in your life in this way will help you let go of stress. When you think about events of the past that cause you stress today, recognize that they were perfect events, events that *could only have occurred in the way they did.* To say it another way, to give up stress, stop punishing yourself and others for "wrongdoings" and "mistakes" of the past. They were the only possibilities.

BRINGING HARMONY TO YOUR ENVIRONMENT

If you would like to bring pleasant, beneficial times into your life, learn to take the stress out of events that happen in your life and in the lives of others. When your friends, mate, or acquaintances do something that seems wrong, let them know that it is "all right." Do it in a way that lets them know you mean it. In my experience, a good way to begin is to say, "It's all right," and then to continue by explaining that your personal philosophy causes you to believe that when an event occurs it's for everyone's complete benefit.

It might take a little time for everyone to see that it was just right, but in the meantime, you have reacted to the situation in a way that lets you experience the good feelings and good effects that come from that type of belief and that type of action. You will be amazed at the result.

If what the person did was not what you wanted, you might want to say to him or her that if a similar event occurs in the future, you would like it handled in a different way. You could even describe what that different way would be. By accepting "what is" and responding from a calm place that does not put a negative label or judgment on the situation or on the people involved, you greatly benefit everyone you come in contact with, and the greatest benefit will be to yourself. Giving up stress will smooth out your life and bring harmony to your environment in a way that will continually amaze and delight you.

When a master passes through an area of conflict, there is a space of peace and harmony surrounding the master. "Who the Master Is" affects all who are near.

A Samurai warrior, a violent man, once approached a great Zen master and belligerently demanded, "Is there a heaven and a hell? And if so, teach me of them!"

The master replied, "What would a stupid Samurai warrior like yourself do with such knowledge?"

The enraged warrior drew his sword and, with a ferocious yell, was sending it on its way to cleave off the master's head when the master held up his hand and said in a calm manner, "Open here the gates of hell."

The Samurai stopped his sword, realizing the great teaching he had just heard and how the master had offered himself to give it. It became crystal clear to him what "hell" was and he was overwhelmed with respect for the master.

He dropped his sword and bowed low before the teacher. Then the master said, "Open here the gates of heaven." At this, the Samurai gave up his warlike ways and became a student of the Zen master.

"Who the Master Is" made such an impression on the warrior that, in an instant, he was transformed. "Who You Are" also transforms others and the world around you—

constantly. It has always been that way. Now you can accomplish the transformation with the full awareness that you are doing it.

Is it tough to keep aware? It's the most difficult job I know of. Answer these two questions aloud: If you could choose to see the events of the past, present, and future as being *completely* beneficial to you, would your stress disappear? Is the choice yours? It feels good to answer yes, doesn't it?

EXERCISE NUMBER ONE

The Only Event Possible

Turn to the page at the end of chapter 5 headed "My Philosophy" (page 99) and in the space below what you wrote earlier, add: *"Every event that occurs is for my greatest benefit—and is the only event possible."*

EXERCISE NUMBER TWO

Perfecting All That Has Gone Before

Find a quiet place where you can be alone and undisturbed for an hour. Sit quietly and think about the events of your life, starting from the time you were a small child. As you come forward in time, recall those times when you did something that was hurtful to another person. (This exercise is similar to the one in chapter 7, but in this case you are calling to mind actions that you took, not things that others did to you that you perceived as hurtful.)

As you recall each incident, see it as "perfect." Mentally, call it "perfect," even though you may still believe the person was hurt by your actions (although by now you should realize the person still benefited by what happened). Realize that, given all that went before and all that did not go before, what happened was the only possibility.

Even though, in the beginning, you may fail to see how the event could have been beneficial in the other person's life, heal your own past by calling the event "perfect." Use all your newfound knowledge to see it that way. You can complete this exercise in two sessions of a half hour each, but make sure they are a full half hour.

During the time you are searching through your memory for hurtful events, if your mind wanders and you think about other kinds of events, estimate the time so spent and add it to the amount of time you will spend in this session. If you need more than one hour, take it or add additional sessions.

You are a pure, bright spirit, here to gain the experiences of this lifetime. Each experience is necessary; each experience takes you to the next level of awareness. You are the sum total of all that has gone before in your life. So taking this time to see as "perfect" all that has gone before is an exercise of major importance, for it will change the sum total of who you are. Do it well and to your complete satisfaction.

EXERCISE NUMBER THREE

Learning to Be Happy—Pleasure Exercise #11

Enjoy another half hour of pleasure. Before choosing your pleasure exercise, think about the other ten pleasure exercises that you have already completed. Pick out the moments when you experienced the most satisfying sense of pleasure.

In choosing this pleasure exercise, let yourself be guided by those special moments. Begin by saying, *"I, [say your name], give myself permission to enjoy a half hour of pleasure."* Do not repeat any of the same pleasure exercises. This exercise can be nearly the same as another one, but vary it in some way.

After the exercise is completed, write a brief summary on the next page under the heading "Pleasure Exercise #11."

Complete the exercises in this chapter before going on to chapter 13.

Pleasure Exercise #11:

Date completed: ______________________________

13

THE PRICE OF FAILURE, THE PRICE OF SUCCESS

To become a champion, fight one more round.
—James J. Corbett (19th-century boxing champion)

YOU KNOW THAT FAILURE MEANS LOSING, but what else does it mean? Put this book down for a moment and think of five things that come under the heading of the price you pay for failure. Write them down on the page at the end of this chapter headed "The Price of Failure" (page 250). Do that before reading on.

Perhaps failing to have enough money prevents you from fulfilling many desires. Perhaps you are unable to do many of the things you want to do. What about loss of self-respect and loss of respect from others, especially your family and friends? What about disillusionment, loss of happiness, and the inability to go where you want, when you want, how you want, and with whom you want? What about feeling unfulfilled or anxious? What about lacking the possessions or the home you want for yourself or your family? The price of failure is mighty high.

Now think of five items that come under the heading of the price you pay for success. Write the ones you can think of on the page at the end of this chapter headed "The Price of Success" (page 251). Do that now.

If you had difficulty in thinking of five items that illustrate the price you pay for success, that's quite natural. If there is a price one pays for success, it is beyond my knowledge. In all the workshops I have given, I have always asked this question about the price of success. I have yet to hear an answer that seems fitting. The usual answer is "hard work," but on the road of success, hard work is actually a benefit rather than a loss.

You might say, "In order to be financially successful, I have paid the price of being away from my family and friends while I was battling it out on the business scene." In reality, that's a price of failure—the price you paid for not being able to earn a living in a way that enabled you to also spend time with your family.

Any "price" you feel you may have paid for achieving any type of success, financial or otherwise, was really a price of failure. Even though you may have achieved your original goal of success, the price you paid in achieving it was the price you paid for failing to be able to do it in a way that allowed you to be successful all along the way. Look at the items you wrote down as being the price of success. Are they the price of success or of failure?

Lao Tzu said this about the person who has made it in life: "He has his yes, he has his no." That means that for the knowledgeable, capable person, "no" results in *being* no, "yes" results in *being* yes. It means being in charge. It means you get to say how it's going to be for you in your life.

THE PATH TO YOUR GOAL

Once you have assimilated the concepts of this program into your mind, your road *to* success will actually be your road *of* success, meaning you will be a success from the moment you begin a project until you achieve your goal. Having the knowledge, the inner certainty that you *will* reach your goal means you already *are* a success. When you have this knowledge, your actions radiate success. All who come in contact with you experience the successful person you are. You can then achieve your goals quickly and advances come rapidly. When a seeming setback comes, you will look at it as one of the necessary occurrences on the way to your successful goal, part of the success rather than the unfortunate mishap it *appears* to be.

In an earlier chapter, I wrote about the making of my film, *Goin' Home*, and running out of money in New Orleans and having to send the crew home. I wrote that I did not intend to quit the project, but instead I had the one-third-finished film edited and took it to England to see if I could arrange for a distribution agreement. So in 1972 I paid a visit to the London offices of Rank Film Distributors, the major film distribution company in England at the time. I was there to talk to the managing director. When I got there, he told me his company would only consider signing a contract to distribute a film after the film was completed and they had seen the finished product.

"Oh, that's terrific," I said. "This will be the first time you'll sign a contract before the film is finished!"

"No, it won't be the first time," he replied, "We just don't do that."

Eight weeks later, the contract was signed. Eight weeks was the time this man needed to get used to the idea of a change in policy. I was patient and persevering. I knew from the beginning what the outcome would be, and I had already experienced the success of the achievement. I didn't know how long it would take, but I knew there were reasons I had to be in London for eight weeks. I didn't know what the reasons were, but I knew that I would find out while I finished the negotiations with the managing director. And I knew that what was important for me was what else would happen during the time of the negotiations. As it turned out, I had some of the most wonderful experiences of my life and I made several friends who have remained friends to this day, several decades later.

As I've said throughout these chapters, once you have committed yourself to achieving your goal and you fully realize that you will attain it, what becomes most important is *the path* to your goal. That's where life unfolds in its moment-by-moment wonderment.

There may be events or situations in your life that you think have been or are currently detrimental to your happiness or to your success. Perhaps you think you read poorly or that in conversation you're less than a dazzling wit, less than an audience charmer. Perhaps you think your looks leave something to be desired or that your personality is unexciting. Maybe you have a physical impairment, you're poor, you have little formal education, or you are or were less than a brilliant student in school. Perhaps at work there are others who seem to get ahead faster than you and you feel that you could, too, if only you were friends with the right people. After all, you've heard the old saying: "It's not what you know but who you know."

If any or all of these feelings and situations exist in your life, this is the time to realize that those supposed handicaps *are a benefit to you*. They are the means by which you will achieve your successes. If you think that you have to become a success *in spite* of them rather than *because* of them, you will forever wander around looking for success, thinking that you are being held back by the very things that have perfectly equipped you to achieve any goal you desire!

BECAUSE OF OBSTACLES, NOT IN SPITE OF THEM

One day I received a letter from a person who had heard an interview I had given on the radio. The letter read: "Hello Chris, my name is Cory. I heard your radio program and was thrilled by it! I, too, used to look at life in much the same way that you do today. I, too, believed that I could have anything I wanted. I was capable and powerful and everything was going my way until I suffered a great tragedy. It is so humiliating, I cannot even tell you about it, not even in a letter. It changed my whole life.

"I am a recluse now and I sit at home much of the time, hoping that no one will find out my secret. I used to have many friends and was considered quite a man about town. That has all changed. Since the terrible event came into my life four years ago, everything has gone wrong. It has left me powerless. I am too embarrassed to tell you what the event was, even though you don't know who I am and will never know who I am.

"I want very much to come and take your workshop, but I cannot do that. You see, I want to be a star, a movie star. I know I have it in me to be that star and if I were to come and take your workshop now and tell you what my terrible secret is, then, when I became a star, you would know my secret and I wouldn't be able to stand the shame of it. I am asking you to give me your workshop over the telephone. I will pay whatever you ask, but my identity must remain a secret. I am a nobody now, but one day I will be a somebody and my secret must remain safe."

I wrote to Cory and said that he could come to the workshop and keep his secret. He called me on the phone and said that he didn't want to do that.

"Cory," I said, "you tell me that you're going to be a great star *in spite of* your great handicap. As long as you continue in that line of thinking, the chances of your becoming a great star are incredibly slim. On the other hand, if you knew that you could become a star *because of your great handicap*, your chances would immediately increase a hundredfold. If you knew that everything that has occurred in your life to this point, including this telephone call, has equipped and prepared you for the stardom you desire, you would be looking at your 'hardship' with new eyes, knowing that it was *an essential part of your stardom*.

"Further, if you knew that all things are possible for those who believe that all things are possible, you would be a star already. Everyone who has that knowledge is already a superstar. What happened in your life is beyond recall because you are unable to roll back time to undo the event and have it happen another way. What you *can* do is to *change the way you look at the event*. Treat what happened as the best thing that could have happened. *Make believe it happened so that you could become a star!* After all, since it's already occurred, that's the only rational option you have if you wish to be successful.

"If you continue to look at what happened as a detriment in your life, an obstacle, that's what it will continue to be. You can change the way you think about it at any moment, including this one. By making a big, bad thing out of what happened, and by keeping it a secret, you *increase* the negative power of the event. What happened to you may, in fact, be very powerful, but you are using its power in a way that works against you and holds you back rather than propelling you forward. Should you achieve stardom, it will be *because* of what happened to you!"

I never heard from Cory again, and I don't know if he ever achieved his longed-for stardom. It is unlikely he achieved his goal because of his view that what had happened to him was an obstacle. Another part of Cory's equation that makes it unlikely he'll achieve his goal is that he was longing for stardom rather than longing to be a great actor, which would result in stardom. To further that thought, don't long to be rich or happy; long to be good enough at something that will enable you to obtain riches and happiness.

There once lived a great prince who was leading his followers against a horde of invaders threatening his little kingdom. One of the prince's soldiers, a young captain, looked enviously over at the prince, who was holding his golden sword aloft, its blade flashing in the sun. The captain said to himself, "If I had a sword like that, I, too, could lead this charge, but all I have is this plain blade!" He angrily snapped his weapon in half across his knee, flung it away from himself, and slunk off the field.

Later in the day, the prince, who had lost his sword in battle, was being driven back by the invaders. As he came upon the spot where the deserting captain had flung his broken sword, he saw it lying in the sand. With a glad cry, he leaped off his horse, grabbed the broken sword, and with it turned and led the charge, achieving a great victory.

What I explained to Cory is what I've been saying over and over in different ways in this book: It's important—no, it's essential—to remember *that the Universe you live in is set up so that everything benefits you completely*. Whatever has happened to you, whatever you are, whoever you are, whatever you have been, whatever you have is exactly what you need in order to become anything and everything you want. *The only thing you need to do is know that and act on it.*

WAS IT BAD OR A BLESSING?

My son Pax and I have learned firsthand that what seems like the hardest and worst of times can turn out to be for our complete benefit. When he was fifteen, Pax began using drugs and alcohol. When Pax was eighteen, he came home from school one day, began crying, and told me he was hooked on heroin. For the next six years, I battled heroin for Pax's life. I put him in thirty-day programs, sixty-day programs, and ninety-day programs. Nothing worked. He was clean forty times or more. It was as if he was powerless to resist the temptation. I was constantly afraid I would lose him, and I never knew from one day to the next if I was going to see him again.

I took him to drug therapists, alcohol therapists, psychologists, psychiatrists, addiction specialists, and counselors of every sort. They all had suggestions for rehab, twelve-step programs, and more counseling, but not one of them was really seeking to discover *why* Pax was using heroin. In nearly every case, their suggestions were directed to creating an environment where he would be less apt to use heroin. They told me to change his circle of friends, take him to twelve-step meetings, and they advised me to punish him for his bad behavior. But we found out that punishment doesn't work as a means to correct substance abuse, even when someone is facing death.

During Pax's ten years of addiction, he stole drugs from a drug dealer in his desperation to get a fix. When the dealer caught him, he drove him into the desert to kill him. He forced him to dig his own grave. Then he threw him in the grave and laid the cold steel of a knife on his belly, preparing to cut him open and leave him as an example to other junkies not to steal from drug dealers. Somehow, Pax talked the dealer out of killing him by convincing him that he could get the money.

The day after that harrowing experience, another dealer Pax had stolen from found him and repeatedly kicked him in the face with his steel-toed boots, breaking his jaw in two places. Pax went to the hospital to get his jaws wired shut. His teeth were pointing in all directions, he was barely able to speak, and he had to sift food through his teeth. He went to his apartment from the hospital and I hurried over to see him. I walked in the door and, unbelievably, at that very moment, he was smoking heroin and using cocaine.

It seemed hopeless. I believed that Pax was turning to heroin for a reason, but I did not know what the reason was. In his drug-free days before he became dependent, he was athletic, outgoing, happy, and a good student, even achieving a student-of-the-month award. He wanted to stop using heroin and cocaine and return to a normal life, but he was unable to stop.

Yet, I never gave up hope. When nothing else worked, we finally created our own holistic, hand-tailored program using a variety of effective therapies. It saved Pax's life. During that whole time, I never stopped encouraging him to keep searching for the real, underlying cause of why he was turning to addictive drugs. One day, at last, Pax discovered the "why" behind his dependency. That was the last day he ever used drugs or alcohol. In that moment, he was able to free himself of his addiction.

Today, Pax is healthy, happy, prosperous, clear minded, and completely cured—and helping others to achieve the same freedom that he has achieved. As you read earlier, he and I founded and are the codirectors of the Passages Addiction Cure Center in Malibu, California. It was Pax's idea to open Passages. When he had finally cured himself of his dependency, he said to me, "Look, we know how to do it—let's do it." At Passages, we use what we learned in curing him to help others discover the underlying causes of their addiction or alcoholism and break free.

To some, Pax's years of addiction and trauma may seem like an irretrievable loss. How could they have been a benefit to him or to me? Yet if you were to ask Pax how he sees the years of his addiction—the beatings, the degradation, the humiliation, the loss of friends, the loss of his college years, the loss of respect, the lost years—he would tell you that it was the most terrible experience of his life and also the greatest. He would tell you that those years led him to his life's work, that without them he would never have had the idea or the drive to create Passages, and that the Universe was preparing him for a brilliant future in which he could help save the lives of hundreds of thousands of lost souls. He would go on to say, and I've heard him say it, that if he had to go through it all again to achieve what he has now achieved, he would do it.

Not only that, but as a result of this experience I was able to write *The Alcoholism and Addiction Cure: A Holistic Approach to Total Recovery* to help others achieve a cure for their dependency on alcohol, prescription medications, street drugs, and addictive behavior. In it, Pax tells his story in detail and I share the keys to recovery we discovered so that people can use these same guidelines to cure themselves. Out of our struggle and trials, we can now give hope and life to millions.

Do we call Pax's long, hard, degrading experience "bad" and "unfortunate" or do we look at the ending it produced and the information it provided and call it a blessing? By now, you must know the answer.

HAVE YOU PAID THE PRICE LONG ENOUGH?

Have you worked at a job that is less than you want long enough? Have you shared a relationship with your mate that has been less than fulfilling long enough? Have you been experiencing mediocre friendships long enough? Have you been less than a good student long enough? Have you been less of the person you know you can be long enough?

One day, when I was visiting the managing director of Rank Film Distributors in London, I struck up a conversation with a young woman who worked there as a typist. She told me she wanted to be a ballerina. I asked her what she was doing working as a typist and she replied that she was earning money to take ballet lessons.

"Why not just go and study with a ballerina?"

"I need to earn the money to pay for the lessons."

"Well," I said in an offhand manner, "I suppose being a ballerina means very little to you."

"Oh no! That's not true. I want to be a ballerina more than anything in the whole world!"

"If that's true, you can begin to take ballet lessons immediately!"

"Oh no! Ballet lessons are very expensive and there is only one woman under whom I want to study!" She named a great prima ballerina who was then teaching in London.

I said, "Look, if you will do what I say, you can begin taking lessons from this wonderful teacher immediately!"

I told her to find the ballet teacher that very day and tell the teacher that more than anything else in the whole world, she wanted to be a ballerina. She would do anything that the ballet teacher asked, if only she could study with her. She would wash floors, mend costumes, work on the sets, do any kind of job at all, as long as she could study with the great teacher. She would also study hard and practice every chance she had, if she could only have the opportunity to dance. Although she was a bit uncertain at first, after we talked more, she agreed to do as I advised.

The next morning, I walked into the office and the girl came over to me, put her arms around my neck, and her eyes filled with tears as she said, "It's all true!"

THE LESSONS THAT GIVE US WISDOM AND STRENGTH

The price that the Universe demands for your success is not what you might think it to be. You might think, "Well, if I work hard enough and long enough, I'll be successful." But that's not the real price, although it may be part of it. The price you have to pay for success is learning the lessons needed to perfect yourself as a human being, a spiritual creature, come to earth for that purpose. The way the Universe perfects us is by putting obstacles in the way of our achieving our desires so we can gain strength and wisdom by overcoming those obstacles.

Here are some examples. Let's say that you are an unforgiving person and the Universe wants you to be more forgiving. It will create a circumstance in your life where you will need the assistance of someone you believe has hurt you, someone you are carrying a grudge against. In order to fulfill your goal, you will have to not only forgive that person but befriend that person so he or she will assist you in your endeavor. Let's say that you're an arrogant person and the Universe wants you to learn humility. It knows that the humble people of our world are well liked and assisted by the rest of us, and the arrogant are disliked and resisted. To achieve your goal, you may feel it is beneath your dignity to ask for help. Therefore, to achieve your goal, you will be forced to ask for help, not once but many times. The result is that you will learn to be humble.

Let's say you're a person who fails to complete projects. In order to achieve success, the Universe will put you in circumstances where you will have to complete projects, because this is the area of weakness in you that must be strengthened if you are to achieve your goals. As many times as you fail to complete your projects, that's how many times the Universe will provide you with new opportunities to complete new projects. And with eternity in which to work, that's a lot of opportunities!

The Universe uses circumstances and people to teach us, and those lessons come to us in many ways. As I said at the beginning of this book, the Universe communicates to us using events. Events are the language of the Universe. The Universe intentionally uses events, and the people involved in those events, to bring us the very information we need to grow and learn and create the life we want.

Twenty some years ago I was having breakfast at my home with my friend Andrew. We were just finishing when he said, "You know, Chris, I have the worst luck picking women. The last nine women I picked all turned out to be bitches." I said, "No, Andrew, that's not right. The last nine women you picked were gentle, good-hearted, warm, loving, wonderful women who you turned into bitches." Andrew got very angry and said, "Who the hell do you think you're talking to?" and angrily stalked out of my house.

Four years later, I received a phone call from him from Hawaii. Andrew told me that he had married, and he and his wife had a son. "I just called to tell you that you were right, and I stopped doing that," he said. Andrew now has three children and is still happily married. The Universe wanted him to get the lesson, and it took nine failed relationships and a message from me before he got it.

THIS IS YOUR TIME

The power to reach your goals lives within you. Remove the limitations you have accepted and you will be drawn to your goals as a stone is drawn to the bottom of a pool. If you say this plan or that idea can fail, you are predicting your own failure.

You began this program because what you had was different from what you wanted and you decided to change that. Well, make the change completely. Carry this book in your hands until you are fully familiar with its concepts. Overcome all that has gone before. Up your ante! You are in control. You are the center from which everything radiates.

I know how hard this is for you. You're like a new blade of grass pushing against the earth, struggling to make its way into the light. Perhaps there is even a small stone right over the spot where you want to emerge. *Supreme effort is required.* But the reward is a life in the sun! The price of failure is too high to pay. The benefits of success are too great to pass by.

This is your time for being strong and persevering. The power is within you. The will is within you. All your effort must be concentrated on persevering. A driveway near my home was recently resurfaced with two inches of blacktop. Three weeks later, a blade of grass pushed its way through! *Success is just as possible for you.*

The Price of Failure:

The Price of Success:

EXERCISE NUMBER ONE

"I Will Persevere"

Get a dictionary and look up the word *persevere*. Do this even if you know the definition. Then, in the space below under the heading "Definition of *Persevere*," write down the definition.

Under the definition, write the following words with conviction, power, and the full force of your will: "I will persevere!" Underline each of the three words separately, and then sign your name.

The Definition of *Persevere*:

Signature: ______________________________

EXERCISE NUMBER TWO

Use What You Are Learning to Help Another

Find a person who needs encouragement and information of the kind you are now able to give and assist that person to discover the concepts you now know. Tell that person that you are doing it as part of a program for personal growth.

A good way to prepare is to reread chapters 1 through 3, taking notes. Use your notes to begin assisting the other person. Explain that he or she could help you by agreeing to let you share concepts from this program. It will be a valuable experience for both of you, and you will be "making it yours" in the most powerful way possible. Do it well and do it to your complete satisfaction. Avoid the attitude "I know more than you."

Your assistance may be required for an extended period of time, but as long as you continue to share your knowledge, you will grow in awareness and capability. It is only necessary that you choose the person and begin to assist him or her before going on to chapter 14.

EXERCISE NUMBER THREE

Seeing "Faults" as Springboards

Sit quietly for a half hour and think of things about yourself that you believe are detrimental, things that you think are holding you back. As you remember each item, smile at it. Realize that it is essential for it to be present in your life. Realize that you need to have the experience of dealing with it. Realize it was one of the essential ingredients that enabled you to arrive at this point in time, where you can have what you want.

Keep at this exercise until you can see that what you previously considered as a fault is actually a springboard for achievement. Should you fail to be able to see these seeming faults as beneficial, read this chapter again and then sit down and evaluate the items once more. It would be better for you to sit there forever than to get up feeling as if you are a victim or have less than you need to achieve what you want.

EXERCISE NUMBER FOUR

Learning to Be Happy—Pleasure Exercise #12

Enjoy another half hour of pleasure. Fulfill this exercise with another person. Be creative, prepare for the occasion thoughtfully, and include another person in making the plan. Discuss what you plan to do with that person to see if he or she can add to the enjoyment. As before, if the pleasure exercise turns out to be less than pleasurable, either begin again or choose another pleasure exercise.

After the exercise is completed, write a brief summary on the next page under the heading "Pleasure Exercise #12."

Complete the exercises in this chapter before going on to chapter 14.

Pleasure Exercise #12:

Date completed: ______________________________

14

OF MAXIMUM IMPORTANCE

If the doors of perception were cleansed,
everything would appear to man as it is, infinite.
—William Blake

YOU ARE NEARING THE END OF THIS BOOK NOW. There's only a little way to go. We have been together just for the time it has taken you to progress to this point. *Having come so far, you have my complete congratulations.* The path you have followed is a solitary path. As you continue to follow this path, merging more of the book's concepts into yourself, *you will become ever more aware, ever more capable.*

Throughout this program, you have learned how to create the world around you and how to obtain what you want. However, in comparison to the time you have spent with this book, you have spent a far greater amount of time living your life before this book came into your hands. I have seen, from careful observation of people "on the path," that unless guidance, inspiration, and encouragement *continue on a daily basis*, their past history clouds their awareness, undermines their gains, and claims their "now." This program is designed to go on as long as you are alive.

It is essential that you nourish yourself each day with the concepts in this book. Therefore, beginning tomorrow, read this book for ten minutes each day for the next 365 days. At the end of each day's reading, mark your place so you will know where to begin the next day. A ribbon is a good way to mark your place.

At the completion of each day's reading, turn to this chapter and read all the paragraphs that begin with the words *Of maximum importance*. Each time you complete the chapters, start over. Keep the concepts alive!

Of maximum importance is that you keep aware of your personal philosophy. It will serve you well through your lifetime.

Of maximum importance is that you keep aware that an event, in itself, is only an event. How you respond to the event determines what it becomes for you. To say that it was perfect, to treat it that way, to recognize that it was the only possibility will keep you experiencing the best of all possible worlds.

Of maximum importance is that you keep aware that all of life is a mirror. "Who You Are" is reflected there. If you are dissatisfied with the reflection, change yourself.

Of maximum importance is that you keep aware that circumstances come into your life so that you can "work out" on them and thereby become more aware and more capable. Confront them. Handle them. Remember, when the path gets tough, you're still on the right track—just a tough track.

Of maximum importance is that you keep aware that you are unique in this world—you are one of a kind. Everything that you perceive is different for you than it is for everyone else. What's true for you may be true only for you. What's true for another may fail to be true for you.

Of maximum importance is that you keep aware that you are the center of your personal Universe, affecting everyone and everything around you.

Of maximum importance is that you participate in life with all you have. Remember, when all the attributes that make up you are in place and operating at peak capacity, you have alloyed those qualities and taken them for your own. You have magnified your potential exponentially. You have strengthened and armored yourself, *and you are of awesome capability*.

Of maximum importance is your knowledge that all things are possible for those who believe that all things are possible. You now know that you are a person who achieves results. When you have decided on a course of action, if it suits your preference to continue on that course, *you will be successful*.

Of maximum importance is that you remember that the power to fulfill every commitment arises within you at the time you make the commitment. You are a "now" person capable of true commitment.

Of maximum importance is that you remember that an end, in itself, is only a symbol of completion. The path that you follow to reach that end is where life unfolds, where capability grows, where knowledge is gained, and where happiness is found.

Of maximum importance is that you keep aware that all of life is a path. Your desires and your circumstances will lead you along that path. Circumstances will force you in a particular direction so that your awareness and capability can grow in a needed way. Following your desires, you will discover an inner well of joy.

Of maximum importance is that you continue to create pleasure for yourself.

Of maximum importance is that when you remember a hurtful incident from the past, done either to you or by you, you immediately heal it by acknowledging its perfection for yourself and for everyone else. Remember the absolute test to determine if something is perfect: *If it happened, it is.*

Of maximum importance is that you keep aware that everything is exactly as it should be and is for your best benefit. It might be that you will want to make changes in the way things are—that's exactly right too.

You have broken loose from that which has bound you. You are a shining, radiant being, gifted with a portion of all the powers of the Universe in this wondrous moment called "now," which is the only time that ever is. It is refreshing to look at the evening sky and see perfection. It is wonderful to look at a vast mountain range or a great ocean and see perfection. Yet, in addition to those things, there are these truths: All the events in your life that have brought you to this moment are perfect. Your being where you are is perfect. Your reading this is perfect. *And you are perfect.*

Love from your friend,

Every ending is a new beginning.

You are never forgotten
but are held at every moment
in the great awareness.
—Ancient wisdom

NOTES

Chapter 2

1. *The Way of Life According to Lao Tzu*, trans. Witter Bynner (New York: Perigee, 1994), 31.

Chapter 4

1. G. Ganis, W. L. Thompson, and S. M. Kosslyn, "Brain Areas Underlying Visual Mental Imagery and Visual Perception: An fMRI Study," *Cognitive Brain Research* 20, no. 2 (2004): 226–41.

2. Norman Doidge, *The Brain That Changes Itself: Stories of Personal Triumph from the Frontiers of Brain Science* (New York: Penguin Books, 2007), 204, 368.

CHRIS PRENTISS is the cofounder and codirector, along with his son Pax, of the world-famous Passages Addiction Cure Center in Malibu, California. He is also the author of the popular *The Alcoholism and Addiction Cure: A Holistic Approach to Total Recovery* and *Zen and the Art of Happiness*, and he has written a dozen books on Chinese philosophy and personal growth under his pen name, Wu Wei. Prentiss has led personal empowerment workshops in Southern California and has written, produced, and directed a feature film. He resides with his wife, Lyn, in Malibu, California.

You can visit his Passages Addiction Cure Center website at www.Passagesmalibu.com. For more information about his books, visit www.PowerPressPublishing.com.